U0018778

你 到 底 是 誰

啟 動 意 識 的 更 高 層 次

當下的覺醒
Stillness Speaks

Eckhart Tolle
艾克哈特·托勒＝著

劉永毅＝譯

CONTENTS

Introduction

目錄

✳前言　找回你內在的平安

　　真正的靈性導師，在一般傳統的文字上，已沒有更多可以傳授的，他無法為你再增加新訊息、新信念或新行為準則，他唯一的功能是幫助你移除那些妨礙你從生命的深處去看清自己本來是誰，去了解自己本來已知道的事。靈性導師的存在，是為了向你揭示內心深處的世界及深邃的平靜。

　　如果你想從一位靈性導師或現在手上這本書裡，尋求有激發性的想法、理論、信念或知性的討論，那你可要失望了。也就是說，如果你想要的是餵養思考的食物，你在這裡不但找不到，同時你會錯失這些教導裡最重要的訊息。本書最重要的訊息不在這些文字裡，而是在你心裡。在閱讀本書時，你要隨時記得，並且去感覺它。文字不過是路標，他們所指向的在你的思維中找不到，只存在於你的內在，在一個比思維更寬闊、更廣袤無垠的空間裡。這裡的特徵是生意盎然的平安，因此，只要你在讀本書時感覺到這股內在平安，這書就在發揮它的作用，完成它做為導師的功能：提醒你「你是誰」，並帶領你回家。

　　這也不是一本逐頁讀完即可束諸高閣的書，要與它活在一起，時常拾起它，不過更重要的是，要時常放下它，或讓自己

捧著它比閱讀它的時間更多。相信許多讀者拿起本書之後，總會自然而然地想要中止閱讀、暫歇、沉思，進而進入靜觀寂照之中。在閱讀的過程中，停下來要比一直讀下去來得更重要，也更有幫助。且讓本書發揮它的功能，將你從不斷重複且受制約的思維夾纏中喚醒吧！

本書的形式可視為是古老印度記載靈性教誨經文的現代再現。「經」是一種充滿能量的真理指引，它以寓義精深的箴言、警語的形式出現，沒有太多概念上的精細討論。《吠陀》（Vedas）*1 以及《奧義書》（Upanishads）*2 即是以早期經文形式記載的聖典，佛陀的法語也是。如果你把耶穌的語錄與生平事蹟的記述從敘事脈絡中抽出，也可以看作是一種經的形式，如同中國古老的智慧書《道德經》一樣。這種形式的優點是簡潔有力，在經文中，看不到非必要的心智思考，經文中所指出但沒說的部分，比說出來的更為重要。本書中近似經文形式的寫作風格，於第一章〈靜謐與寂照〉中尤為明顯。這一章的文句最是簡潔，它含括了全書的精義，也可能是部分讀者所需求的全部，其他章節則是為了那些需要更多路標的讀者而寫的。

一如古老的經文，本書所書寫的文字是神聖的，是來自於

一種我們或可稱之為「靜觀寂照」*3的意識狀態。然而，與古老經文不同的是，它們不屬於任何一種宗教或靈修傳統，而是全人類都可以立即感受領略的。此外，本書也提及了另一個迫在眉睫的觀念，那就是人類共同意識的轉化不再是奢侈之舉，也就是說，它不再是少數人的福祉。如果人類不希望自我毀滅，那麼意識的轉化便是必要的。此時此刻，舊有意識的運作無方與新意識的出現正同時在發生。矛盾的是，事情似乎同時在變好與變壞，只是變壞的部分因它製造了許多的「噪音」，而變得更為明顯。

　　當然了，本書採用文字以便閱讀，再轉化為你心智上的思考。但是，這些思考與那些反覆、嘈雜、自私、喋喋不休只為引你注意的一般想法並不相同。如同那些真正的靈性導師，或是古老的經文，存於本書中的文字道理並不會要求你：「看著我。」而是希望你：「超越我。」因為這些思維來自於靜觀寂照，它們擁有的力量，可以引領你回到它們所生起的寂照之中。那寂照是內在的深邃平安，而這些寂照與平安正是你本體的核心要素，未來將拯救並轉化整個世界的就是這個靜觀寂照。

＊1──《吠陀》Vedas

《吠陀》（Vedas）是印度最古代的宗教文獻和文學作品的總稱，是最古老的聖典，也是哲學宗教的起源。「吠陀」是「知識」的意思，婆羅門教認為這是古聖人受神的啟示（Sruti）而寫出來的。《吠陀》共有四種，即《梨俱吠陀》（Rgveda）、《夜柔吠陀》（Yajurveda）、《沙麿吠陀》（Samaveda）、《阿闥婆吠陀》（Atharvaveda），合稱「四吠陀」。

＊2──《奧義書》Upanishads

《奧義書》（Upanishads）又音譯為《優波尼沙》，或意譯為《近坐書》，它是《吠陀》後期探討祭神哲學意義的著作，列為《六吠陀》中的第六部，又稱為《吠檀多》。它成書於《吠陀》的後期，包括150多篇哲學方面的著作，多是大師以智慧傳授學生的語錄，與《論語》頗為類似，集合了各聖賢的集體智慧結晶與吉光片語的意見、看法和教訓，以散文或詩的形式寫出。這些論述天馬行空，影響印度後世唯心論哲學與唯物論哲學觀，對佛學思想也有很大影響。

＊3──靜觀寂照 stillness

「stillness」的直接翻譯有「靜止、不動、平靜、寂靜」等義。可是作者艾克哈特在本書中對此字之使用超過這些意義。在書裡首頁，艾克哈特自己給「stillness」下了定義：它是一種內在空間或察覺知曉的能力。因為有這能力，你對本頁文字才能感知，並轉為種種念頭。沒有這覺曉能力，也就沒有了感覺、思考，甚至世界。顯然艾克哈特所說的「stillness」是在寂靜中保持覺察，因為有這察能力的觀照，萬物才得以顯現，因此本書中採用「靜觀寂照」來對應「stillness」，並以「寂照」使用最為頻繁。

靜謐與寂照

Silence & Stillness

1

When you lose touch with inner stillness, you lose touch with yourself. When you lose touch with yourself, you lose yourself in the world.

Your innermost sense of self, of who you are, is inseparable from stillness. This is the *I Am* that is deeper than name and form.

∫

Stillness is your essential nature. What is stillness? The inner space or awareness in which the words on this page are being perceived and become thoughts. Without that awareness, there would be no perception, no thoughts, no world.

You are that awareness, disguised as a person.

∫

The equivalent of external noise is the inner noise of thinking. The equivalent of external silence is inner stillness.

Whenever there is some silence around you — listen to it. That means just notice it. Pay attention to it. Listening to

　　當你與內在寂照失去了連繫，你便與自己失去了連繫。當你與自己失去了連繫，你便在這世界中丟失了自己。

　　你內心最深處的自我感，對於「我是誰」的認知，與寂照是密不可分的。寂照即是遠比名稱或肉體形相更為底層的「我本是」。

$$\int$$

　　寂照是你的本質天性，它是什麼呢？它是一種內在空間或察覺知曉的能力。因為有它，你對本頁文字才能感知，並轉為種種念頭。沒有這覺曉能力，也就沒有了感覺、思考，甚至世界。

　　你就是那個覺知──只是化裝成人的形相出現。

$$\int$$

　　內在思維的嘈雜與外界的喧囂是等量齊觀的；內在的寂照與外界的靜謐也是如此。

　　無論何時，當你的周遭有那絲靜謐時，傾聽它──僅只覺

silence awakens the dimension of stillness within yourself, because it is only through stillness that you can be aware of silence.

See that in the moment of noticing the silence around you, you are not thinking. You are aware, but not thinking.

∫

When you become aware of silence, immediately there is that state of inner still alertness. You are present. You have stepped out of thousands of years of collective human conditioning.

∫

Look at a tree, a flower, a plant. Let your awareness rest upon it. How still they are, how deeply rooted in Being. Allow nature to teach you stillness.

察它、關注它。傾聽這絲靜謐,將喚醒你內在的寂照,因為唯有透過寂照,你才能覺察到那絲靜謐。

在你留意身邊那絲靜謐時,注意,那一刻你並沒有在進行思考。你在覺察,但沒有在思考。

一旦你開始覺察到靜謐,你便立即進入了內在寂止的警醒狀態,你「臨在」了,同時你也跨出了人類數千年來的集體制約。

凝視一棵樹、一朵花、一株植物,讓覺察停留在那裡。它們是如此地寂靜,如此深刻地根植於本體之上,讓大自然來教導你何謂「寂照」吧!

∫

When you look at a tree and perceive its stillness, you become still yourself. You connect with it at a very deep level. You feel a oneness with whatever you perceive in and through stillness. Feeling the oneness of yourself with all things is true love.

∫

Silence is helpful, but you don't need it in order to find stillness. Even when there is noise, you can be aware of the stillness underneath the noise, of the space in which the noise arises. That is the inner space of pure awareness, consciousness itself.

You can become aware of awareness as the background to all your sense perceptions, all your thinking. Becoming aware of awareness is the arising of inner stillness.

∫

當你凝視著一棵樹，並感知其寂照之際，你自己也將變得靜寂，你與那樹將在極深處產生連結。當你處於寂照之中，並透過寂照去感知一切事物時，你將感覺與感知對象合而為一；這種與萬物一體的感覺，就是真愛。

要尋覓寂照，靜謐可以幫得上忙，但並不是非它不可。即使眾聲喧嘩，你依然可以覺察到那嘈雜下的寂照，覺察到那噪音生起之空間，那裡是你內在的純然覺性，即意識所在之空間。

你將覺察到覺性是你所有感官知覺與念頭的背景，而能夠有此覺察，就是內在寂照的生起。

Any disturbing noise can be as helpful as silence. How? By dropping your inner resistance to the noise, by allowing it to be as it is, this acceptance also takes you into that realm of inner peace that is stillness.

Whenever you deeply accept this moment as it is — no matter what form it takes — you are still, you are at peace.

Pay attention to the gap — the gap between two thoughts, the brief, silent space between words in a conversation, between the notes of a piano or flute, or the gap between the in-breath and out-breath.

When you pay attention to those gaps, awareness of "something" becomes — just awareness. The formless dimension of pure consciousness arises from within you and replaces identification with form.

靜謐可以幫你找到寂照，擾人的噪音一樣也可以。怎麼說呢？只要你能把對噪音的那份抗拒放下，接納噪音就是噪音，這份接納就會把你帶進內在平安之境——寂照。

任何時候，當你全然地接納當下的如實狀態，不管出現的是什麼樣的情況，你都能夠平心靜氣。

請留意間隙，譬如兩個念頭之間的空白，或一段對話之中語詞間短暫的靜默，鋼琴或長笛演奏時音符之間的休止，乃至是一呼一吸之間的停頓。

當你注意到這些間隙時，覺察到「什麼」將僅只是覺察。無形、無相的純粹意識層面將從你內在生起，取代了你原本對於「形相」*的認同。

＊形相 form
「form」做名詞用時，一般將它翻譯成「形狀」或「形相」，經常用來指稱一個物體的物理體態。但是在本書中，作者對「form」一字的使用指涉的範圍更為廣泛，除了物理體態之外，它可以是抽象思維與情緒上的「form」，因此，舉凡物體、情緒、念頭、反應等等，所有能被「覺性」感知到的「對象」，無論具有或不具有物理體態，都算是「form」的一種。在中文中難有適切的字來對應，因此只能就上下文來選擇使用字眼。

True intelligence operates silently. Stillness is where creativity and solutions to problems are found.

∫

Is stillness just the absence of noise and content? No, it is intelligence itself — the underlying consciousness out of which every form is born. And how could that be separate from who you are? The form that you think you are came out of that and is being sustained by it.

It is the essence of all galaxies and blades of grass; of all flowers, trees, birds, and all other forms.

∫

Stillness is the only thing in this world that has no form. But then, it is not really a thing, and it is not of this world.

真正的本智*是默默在運行的。在寂照中，你可以找到解決問題的方法和創造力。

∫

難道寂照就只是無聲、無物嗎？不，它是本智本身——它是藏在萬相之下的意識，所以，它怎能與真正的你有所分離呢？你所認為的這個有形有相的你，也是源自於它、仰賴著它才得以存在。

它也是所有星系、草葉、花朵、樹木、鳥禽與萬相的本質。

∫

寂照是這個世上唯一不具形相的「東西」，事實上，它也不是「東西」，它不屬於這個世界。

＊本智（或智性）intelligence
「intelligence」原有「智能、智慧、理解力」之意，但都容易產生誤解為小我心智的能力，因此本書採用「本智」，取其「生命本然的智慧」之意，以避免被誤會為小我的智能。

∫

When you look at a tree or a human being in stillness, who is looking? Something deeper than the person. Consciousness is looking at its creation.

In the Bible, it says that God created the world and saw that it was good. That is what you see when you look from stillness without thought.

∫

Do you need more knowledge? Is more information going to save the world, or faster computers, more scientific or intellectual analysis? Is it not wisdom that humanity needs most at this time?

But what is wisdom and where is it to be found? Wisdom comes with the ability to be still. Just look and just listen. No more is needed. Being still, looking, and listening activates the non- conceptual intelligence within you. Let stillness direct your words and actions.

∫

　　當你在寂照中凝視著一棵樹或一個人時,是誰在觀看呢?
是某個比你這個人更為深沉的什麼在觀看,是意識在觀看它的
創作。

　　《聖經‧創世記》中提及,神創造了世界,並看著一切所
造的都甚好,當你透過寂照觀看而不起念頭時,你所看見的正
是神所看見的那個「好」。

∫

　　你需要更多的知識嗎?更多的資訊、更快速的電腦、更多
的科學或知性分析,可以拯救世界嗎?此時此刻,人類此刻最
需要的難道不是智慧嗎?

　　但什麼是智慧?何處可以找到它?智慧隨著靜觀寂照的能
力一起出現,只要保持寂照,單純地看和聽,便足以啟動你內
在那無概念的本智。且讓寂照導引你的一言一行吧!

超越心智思維

Beyond the Thinking Mind

2

The human condition: lost in thought.

∫

Most people spend their entire life imprisoned within the confines of their own thoughts. They never go beyond a narrow, mind-made, personalized sense of self that is conditioned by the past.

In you, as in each human being, there is a dimension of consciousness far deeper than thought. It is the very essence of who you are. We may call it presence, awareness, the unconditioned consciousness. In the ancient teachings, it is the Christ within, or your Buddha nature.

Finding that dimension frees you and the world from the suffering you inflict on yourself and others when the mind-made "little me" is all you know and runs your life. Love, joy, creative expansion, and lasting inner peace cannot come into your life except through that unconditioned dimension of consciousness.

If you can recognize, even occasionally, the thoughts that go through your mind as simply thoughts, if you can witness your own mental-emotional reactive patterns as they happen, then that dimension is already emerging in you as the awareness in which thoughts and emotions happen — the timeless inner space in which the content of your life unfolds.

人類的現狀是：迷失在思考之中。

$\int$

多數人一輩子被囚禁在自我設限的思維之中，他們從未跨越那狹隘的、由心智所打造、個人化的自我認知——這被過去制約的自我認知。

在你身上，一如在每個人身上，有個遠比思維更為深邃的意識層面。那就是真正的你的核心本質，我們可稱之為「臨在」、「覺性」，或「不受制約的意識」。在古老的教義之中，它就是你心中的神性或佛性。

找到那意識層面，將使你和整個世界從受苦中解脫。那痛苦是你強加於自己和他人身上的，因為心智所造的「小我」，是你唯一認知的，並掌控了你的生命。愛、喜悅、創意的延伸，以及心中長久的平靜，都必須透過那不受過去制約的意識層面，才能進入你的生命。

如果你能認出，自己心頭一閃而過的念頭純粹就只是念頭，如果你能在自己情緒反應的當下，認出它發生的慣性模式，那即使只是偶然做到，那個有意識的層面已然在你內在以覺性浮現了，念頭與情緒就是從覺性中生起的——在這個沒有時間性的內在空間裡，你生命的種種內容就是在這裡展現。

∫

The stream of thinking has enormous momentum that can easily drag you along with it. Every thought pretends that it matters so much. It wants to draw your attention in completely.

Here is a new spiritual practice for you: don't take your thoughts too seriously.

∫

How easy it is for people to become trapped in their conceptual prisons.

The human mind, in its desire to know, understand, and control, mistakes its opinions and viewpoints for the truth. It says: this is how it is. You have to be larger than thought to realize that however you interpret "your life" or someone else's life or behavior, however you judge any situation, it is no more than a viewpoint, one of many possible perspectives. It is no more than a bundle of thoughts. But reality is one unified whole, in which all things are interwoven, where nothing exists in and by itself. Thinking fragments reality — it cuts it up into conceptual bits and pieces.

∫

　　思緒之流擁有極大的動能，可以輕易地拖著你與它同行。每個想法都假裝自己是如此地重要，這樣才可以獲得你全部的注意。

　　提供你一個新的靈修練習：對你的想法別太認真。

∫

　　人們多麼輕易地就掉入自己的概念牢籠之中。

　　由於想知道、明白與想控制的種種欲望，心智把自己的意見與觀點誤認為是真相。心智說：事情是這樣、這樣的；所以，你得比你的心智所想的更為宏觀才能明白，無論你如何詮釋「你的生命」，或他人的生命、行為，你對任何情況的意見或看法，也都不過就是一種見解，是諸多可能的看法之一，最多也不過就是一堆思緒。但「真實」是一個整體的存在，這裡面所有事物是交織的，沒有一件可以獨自存在。思考碎裂了「真實」，將它切成了無數的概念碎片。

The thinking mind is a useful and powerful tool, but it is also very limiting when it takes over your life completely, when you don't realize that it is only a small aspect of the consciousness that you are.

∫

Wisdom is not a product of thought. The deep *knowing* that is wisdom arises through the simple act of giving someone or something your full attention. Attention is primordial intelligence, consciousness itself. It dissolves the barriers created by conceptual thought, and with this comes the recognition that nothing exists in and by itself. It joins the perceiver and the perceived in a unifying field of awareness. It is the healer of separation.

∫

Whenever you are immersed in compulsive thinking, you are avoiding what is. You don't want to be where you are. Here, Now.

　　會思考的心智是一種強而有力的工具，但是當你沒有認識到它只是意識的一小部分，而讓它完全掌控你的生命時，它反而會是局限的。

　　智慧並非思考下的產物。智慧是深刻的「了知」，你只要單純的做一件事——全心注意著某人或某事，「了知」就會生起。專注是本初的智性，是意識本身。它消除了概念化思維所形成的阻礙，於是你認清了沒有任何事物可以獨立存在。在覺性之中，專注讓感知者與被感知對象合而為一，專注是你我分別的療癒師。

　　每當你沉溺在強迫性思維裡，你便是在迴避事情的實際情況，你不想處於你所在之處——此地、此刻。

Dogmas — religious, political, scientific— arise out of the erroneous belief that thought can encapsulate reality or the truth. Dogmas are collective conceptual prisons. And the strange thing is that people love their prison cells because they give them a sense of security and a false sense of "I know."

Nothing has inflicted more suffering on humanity than its dogmas. It is true that every dogma crumbles sooner or later, because reality will eventually disclose its falseness; however, unless the basic delusion of it is seen for what it is, it will be replaced by others.

What is this basic delusion? Identification with thought.

Spiritual awakening is awakening from the dream of thought.

∫

　　宗教、政治或科學上的教條，皆源於人們的錯誤信念——相信思想可以涵括真理或事實。這些教條就像集合式的觀念牢籠，奇怪的是，人們卻喜愛這些囚室，只因它們帶來安全感，以及一種假象的「我知道」。

　　沒有任何東西比教條在人類身上所造成的痛苦更多。事實上，每個教條早晚都會崩解，因為「真實」最後一定會揭穿它虛假的面目；然而，除非人們看穿教條虛妄的本質，否則舊教條將只是被另一個新教條取代罷了。

　　何謂教條虛妄的本質呢？那就是認同於思維。

∫

　　靈性的覺醒，指的是從思維之夢中醒來。

∫

The realm of consciousness is much vaster than thought can grasp. When you no longer believe everything you think, you step out of thought and see clearly that the thinker is not who you are.

∫

The mind exists in a state of "not enough" and so is always greedy for more. When you are identified with mind, you get bored and restless very easily. Boredom means the mind is hungry for more stimulus, more food for thought, and its hunger is not being satisfied.

When you feel bored, you can satisfy the mind's hunger by picking up a magazine, making a phone call, switching on the TV, surfing the web, going shopping, or — and this is not uncommon — transferring the mental sense of lack and its need for *more* to the body and satisfy it briefly by ingesting more food.

Or you can stay bored and restless and observe what it feels like to be bored and restless. As you bring awareness to the feeling, there is suddenly some space and stillness around it, as it were. A little at first, but as the sense of inner

　　意識所能覺察的範圍，遠比思維所能理解的更為浩瀚廣闊。當你不再相信你所想的每件事，你便跨出了思維，並清楚知道那位「思考者」並非是真正的你。

$$\int$$

　　心智常處於「不滿足」的狀態之中，因此它總是貪得無厭。當你認同於心智時，你很容易覺得無聊與不安，無聊代表著心智渴求更多的刺激，更多填飽思考欲求的糧食，它的飢渴還沒被滿足。

　　當你覺得無聊時，可以隨手拿起一本雜誌，打通電話、轉換電視頻道、漫遊網路、逛逛街；或者，更常見的方法是大吃一頓，暫時以身體上的口欲，來滿足精神上的匱乏欲求。

　　然而，你也可以保持無聊與不安，並觀察這無聊與不安是什麼樣的感受。當你帶著覺性去觀察感受時，剎那間，某些空間與寂照會在感受四周生起。它一直都在那兒，起初並不明顯，但隨著心中空間感的不斷增長，無聊的感受將開始消失，並不再那麼明顯與強烈。所以，即使只是無聊，都可以教導你認識「你是誰」與「你不是誰」。

space grows, the feeling of boredom will begin to diminish in intensity and significance. So even boredom can teach you who you are and who you are not.

You discover that a "bored person" is not who you are. Boredom is simply a conditioned energy movement within you. Neither are you an angry, sad, or fearful person. Boredom, anger, sadness, or fear are not "yours," not personal. They are conditions of the human mind. They come and go.

Nothing that comes and goes is you. "I am bored." Who knows this? "I am angry, sad, afraid." Who knows this? You are the knowing, not the condition that is known.

Prejudice of any kind implies that you are identified with the thinking mind. It means you don't see the other human being anymore, but only your own concept of that human being. To reduce the aliveness of another human being to a concept is already a form of violence.

你將發現，「無聊的人」並非是「你」。無聊僅只是你體內一股受限的能量流動。相同地，你也不是一個愛生氣、悲傷或滿懷恐懼的人。無聊、生氣、悲傷或恐懼，既不屬於你，也不是你個人所特有。它們是人類的心智狀態，總是來來去去、變化不斷。

那些來去的，都不是你。

「我很無聊。」誰是那個知道「無聊」的人？

「我很生氣、悲傷、害怕。」誰是那個知道「生氣」、「悲傷」、「害怕」的人？

你就是那個「知道」，而不是那些被知道的情緒狀態。

任何偏見，皆意味著你認同於思考的心智。這也意味著在你眼中，不再看不見其他人，但只有概念認知上所謂的「人」。將活生生的人簡化為一個概念，已經是某種形式的暴力了。

Thinking that is not rooted in awareness becomes self-serving and dysfunctional. Cleverness devoid of wisdom is extremely dangerous and destructive. That is the current state of most of humanity. The amplification of thought as science and technology, although intrinsically neither good nor bad, has also become destructive because so often the thinking out of which it comes has no roots in awareness.

The next step in human evolution is to transcend thought. This is now our urgent task. It doesn't mean not to think anymore, but simply not to be completely identified with thought, possessed by thought.

$$\int$$

Feel the energy of your inner body. Immediately mental noise slows down or ceases. Feel it in your hands, your feet, your abdomen, your chest. Feel the life that you are, the life that animates the body.

The body then becomes a doorway, so to speak, into a deeper sense of aliveness underneath the fluctuating emotions and underneath your thinking.

$$\int$$

　　思考若非植基於覺性，將變得自私與功能障礙。沒有智慧的聰明是非常危險，且具有毀滅性的，然而，這卻是目前大多數人類的狀態。思維會以科學與科技的形式不斷地擴大，本質上這無所謂好壞，然而，當有太多是出於缺乏覺性的思考時，也可以變得具有毀滅性。

　　人類進化的下一步，將是超越思維的局限，這是我們的當務之急。但這不是說人類不再去思考，而只是希望人類不要全然認同於思維，而被思維所掌控。

　　感受你內在的能量，腦中的雜音便會立刻慢下來或停止。在你的雙手、雙腳、腹部與胸部上去感受它，感受你本然的生命，那讓肉體活起來的生命。

　　身體於是變成了一扇門，通過它你可以更深刻地去感受，那潛藏於你不安的情緒與思維底下活著的感覺。

There is an aliveness in you that you can feel with your entire Being, not just in the head. Every cell is alive in that presence in which you don't need to think. Yet, in that state, if thought is required for some practical purpose, it is there. The mind can still operate, and it operates beautifully when the greater intelligence that you *are* uses it and expresses itself through it.

∫

You may have overlooked that brief periods in which you are "conscious without thought" are already occurring naturally and spontaneously in your life. You may be engaged in some manual activity, or walking across the room, or waiting at the airline counter, and be so completely present that the usual mental static of thought subsides and is replaced by an aware presence. Or you may find yourself looking at the sky or listening to someone without any inner mental commentary. Your perceptions become crystal clear, unclouded by thought.

To the mind, all this is not significant, because it has "more important" things to think about. It is also not memorable, and that's why you may have overlooked that it is already happening.

　　你的內在，有種可以以你全然的本體（而非只是頭腦）去感受的活潑生命。「臨在」的當下，身體的每個細胞都是活的，你不需要思考。然而，在此狀態中，如果為了某些實際的需要你必須思考，心智就在那兒，仍可運作，而且可以完美地運作，因為更大的本初智性——真正的你，在啟用著心智，並透過心智來表現其自身。

$$\int$$

　　你也許忽略了在你生命裡，曾經瞬間閃過一些「不思而察」的片刻，當時你也許正從事著某種體能活動，或是走過房間，或是在航空公司櫃檯前排隊等候，由於你全然地「臨在」，平日紛起的思緒沉澱了下來，取而代之的是一種有覺知的「臨在」。也許你曾經發現自己正凝視天空或傾聽他人說話，但腦中不起一絲意見，你的感知如水晶般清澈，不為念頭之雲所遮蔽。

　　對心智而言，這些片刻並不重要，因為還有「更重要的」事情得去思考。它們是如此地短暫且無從記憶，以致雖然已發生，你卻沒能覺察。

The truth is that it is the most significant thing that *can* happen to you. It is the beginning of a shift from thinking to aware presence.

∫

Become at ease with the state of "not knowing." This takes you beyond mind because the mind is always trying to conclude and interpret. It is afraid of not knowing. So, when you can be at ease with not knowing, you have already gone beyond the mind. A deeper knowing that is non- conceptual then arises out of that state.

∫

Artistic creation, sports, dance, teaching, counseling — mastery in any field of endeavor implies that the thinking mind is either no longer involved at all or at least is taking second place. A power and intelligence greater than you and yet one with you in essence takes over. There is no decision-making process anymore; spontaneous right action happens, and "you" are not doing it. Mastery of life is the opposite of control. You become aligned with the greater consciousness. *It* acts, speaks, does the works.

　　事實是，這些短暫片刻才是你生命中能發生的最有意義的事。它們是從思考轉化到有覺知「臨在」的開端。

$$\int$$

　　面對「未知」要處之泰然，這會帶領你超越心智的局限。因為心智總喜歡推斷與詮釋，它害怕「未知」，所以，當你可以寬心面對「未知」，你就已然超越心智，而一種更深沉、非概念化的「了知」，也將從這裡面生起。

$$\int$$

　　想要在藝術創作、運動、舞蹈、教學、諮商的領域中有所專精，需要的是努力，這也意味著思考的心智完全不需要介入，或至少是次要的。當一切皆由一個遠超過你，但本質上與你合一的力量與本智接掌時，就再也沒有什麼決定要做了，但你卻可以臨場適恰地隨機反應，這都不是「你」在做。掌握生命與控制它是對立的，你要與更廣闊的意識合而為一，讓「它」採取行動、發表言論、完成工作。

∫

A moment of danger can bring about a temporary cessation of the stream of thinking and thus give you a taste of what it means to be present, alert, aware.

∫

The Truth is far more all-encompassing than the mind could ever comprehend. No thought can encapsulate the Truth. At best, it can point to it. For example, it can say: "All things are intrinsically one." That is a pointer, not an explanation. Understanding these words means *feeling* deep within you the truth to which they point.

∫

危險出現時，思維之流會短暫中止，在此間隙中，你將品嘗到何謂「臨在」、「警覺」與「覺察」。

∫

真理遠比心智所能理解的更為全面。思維是無法涵蓋真理的，最多只能指向真理，譬如思維可以說「萬物在本質上是一體的」，但它只是個指標，並非一個明白的解釋，想要懂得這句話的意思，你得在內心真正感受這句話所指涉的真理。

小我
The Egoic Self

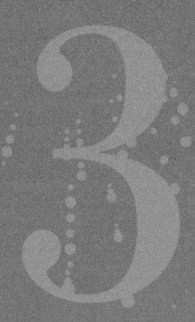

The mind is incessantly looking not only for food for thought; it is looking for food for its identity, its sense of self. This is how the ego comes into existence and continuously re-creates itself.

∫

When you think or speak about yourself, when you say, "I," what you usually refer to is "me and my story." This is the "I" of your likes and dislikes, fears and desires, the "I" that is never satisfied for long. It is a mind-made sense of who you are, conditioned by the past and seeking to find its fulfillment in the future.

Can you see that this "I" is fleeting, a temporary formation, like a wave pattern on the surface of the water?

Who is it that sees this? Who is it that is *aware* of the fleetingness of your physical and psychological form? I Am. This is the deeper "I" that has nothing to do with past and future.

∫

　　心智不停地尋找思維的糧食，也不停地尋找自我認同的糧
食，「小我」因而誕生，並不斷地再創自己。

　　當你想到或談到自己，說到「我」這個字時，通常你說的
是「我和我的故事」。這個以你自己的好惡、恐懼與欲望為中
心的「我」，是永遠無法真正被滿足的。這個由心智所打造所
謂的「我」，受到了過去的制約，並企求在未來得到滿足。

　　你能明白這個「我」是飛逝的，是一個暫時的構成狀態，
就像水面掀起的波紋嗎？

　　那個能看明此事的人是誰？那個能覺察到肉體與心理的存
在形式是暫時性的人是誰？是「我本是」，它才是更深處那個
與過去或未來無關的「我」。

What will be left of all the fearing and wanting associated with your problematic life situation that every day takes up most of your attention? A dash — one or two inches long, between the date of birth and date of death on your gravestone.

To the egoic self, this is a depressing thought. To you, it is liberating.

When each thought absorbs your attention completely, it means you identify with the voice in your head. Thought then becomes invested with a sense of self. This is the ego, the mind-made "me." That mentally constructed self feels incomplete and precarious. That's why fearing and wanting are its predominant emotions and motivating forces.

When you recognize that there is a voice in your head that pretends to be you and never stops speaking, you are awakening out of your unconscious identification with the stream of thinking. When you notice that voice, you realize that who you are is not the voice — the thinker — but the one who is aware of it.

Knowing yourself as the awareness behind the voice is freedom.

　　人生充滿困境，它耗去了我們絕大部分的關注，請問除了經常伴隨在困境裡的恐懼與欲望外，你的人生還剩下什麼？一個破折號，一個只有一、兩英寸長的破折號，刻在你的墓碑上生年與死期之間。

　　對小我而言，這聽來沮喪，但對你來說，卻是種解放。

　　當每個念頭都能完全地抓住你的注意時，便意味著你向腦海中浮現的那個聲音認同了，於是這些念頭將充滿自我感，這就是小我，一個由心智所打造的「我」。這個由心智所建構的自我，感覺上並不完整也不穩定，因此，恐懼與欲望才成了它最主要的情緒與驅動力量。

　　當你認出腦海中有個聲音假裝是你，叨叨絮絮地說個不停，你便已然從自己無意識下所認同的思緒之流裡醒過來了。當你注意到那聲音，你就會明白真正的你並非那聲音（思考者），而是覺察那聲音的人。

　　知道你自己就是那隱於聲音之後的覺性，那就是自由。

The egoic self is always engaged in seeking. It is seeking more of this or that to add to itself, to make itself feel more complete. This explains the ego's compulsive preoccupation with future.

Whenever you become aware of yourself "living for the next moment," you have already stepped out of that egoic mind pattern, and the possibility of choosing to give your full attention to this moment arises simultaneously.

By giving your full attention to this moment, an intelligence far greater than the egoic mind enters your life.

∫

When you live through the ego, you always reduce the present moment to a means to an end. You live for the future, and when you achieve your goals, they don't satisfy you, at least not for long.

When you give more attention to the doing than to the future result that you want to achieve through it, you break the old egoic conditioning. Your doing then becomes not only a great deal more effective, but infinitely more fulfilling and joyful.

　　小我總是尋尋覓覓著，希望找到更多的這個、那個，來為自己增添份量，讓自己感覺更為完整；也因此，小我總是強迫性地被未來所佔滿。

　　無論何時，只要你能覺察到自己正在「為下一刻而活」，你便已跨越了小我心智的模式，同一時間，你想把全部注意力投注在當下的可能性也出現了。

　　只要你把全部的注意力投注在此時此刻，一個遠比小我心智更為寬廣宏大的智性，便進入了你的生命。

　　只要你活在小我之中，便總會將當下此刻矮化為達成目標的工具。你為了未來而活，然而即使你達成了目標，它們卻依然無法滿足你，至少撐不了太久。

　　當你專注於手上的事情，而不是花心思去想它未來可以達到怎樣的成果，你便已擺脫了舊有的小我制約模式。於是，手上的這件工作，不但會進行得更有效率，還會帶給你極大的滿足與喜悅。

∫

Almost every ego contains at least an element of what we might call "victim identity." Some people have such a strong victim image of themselves that it becomes the central core of their ego. Resentment and grievances form an essential part of their sense of self.

Even if your grievances are completely "justified," you have constructed an identity for yourself that is much like a prison whose bars are made of thought forms. See what you are doing to yourself, or rather what your mind is doing to you. Feel the emotional attachment you have to your victim story and become aware of the compulsion to think or talk about it. Be there as the witnessing presence of your inner state. You don't have to *do* anything. With awareness comes transformation and freedom.

∫

幾乎所有的小我，至少都包含了一個所謂「受害者認同」的成分。有些人對於自己抱著極為強烈的受害者形象，這形象變成了他們小我的核心，怨恨與牢騷成了他們自我感的主要成分。

　　即使你的牢騷不滿聽來完全「合理」，你已在為自己建構一個牢籠般的身分，你種種的念頭就是這牢籠的柵欄。與其說「看看你把自己怎麼了」，還不如說「看看你的心智把你怎麼了」。試著去感受，自己在情緒上對於受害者故事的執著，試著在自己強迫性地想到它、談論它時，開始去覺察它，有如現場目擊證人般地覺察著你的內在狀態，你不需要有任何作為，因為覺知會帶來轉化與自由。

Complaining and reactivity are favorite mind patterns through which the ego strengthens itself. For many people, a large part of their mental- emotional activity consists of complaining and reacting against this or that. By doing this, you make others or a situation "wrong" and yourself "right." Through being "right," you feel superior, and through feeling superior, you strengthen your sense of self. In reality, of course, you are only strengthening the illusion of ego.

Can you observe those patterns within yourself and recognize the complaining voice in your head for what it is?

∫

The egoic sense of self needs conflict because its sense of a separate identity gets strengthened in fighting against this or that, and in demonstrating that this is "me" and that is not "me."

Not infrequently, tribes, nations, and religions derive a strengthened sense of collective identity from having enemies. Who would the "believer" be without the "unbeliever" ?

∫

　　抱怨與唱反調，是小我最常用來鞏固自身的心智模式。對多數人來說，他們經常有的情緒行為就是抱怨與反抗這個或那個。他們用這樣的動作，來標舉出別人或某一情況是「錯」的，以彰顯自己是「對」的，並因為自己是「對」的，而感覺高人一等，從而加強了自我感。實際上，這只是徒然強化小我的假象罷了。

　　你能觀察自己內在的這些心智模式嗎？你能認清腦海中浮現的種種抱怨之聲究竟是什麼嗎？

　　小我的自我感需要衝突，因為透過對抗，以及強調「這是我」與「這不是我」的分別，小我得以強化自己的個別性身分。

　　部落、國家與宗教之間，藉由敵人的存在，形成一鞏固的集體認同，這樣的情形並非罕見。試問如果沒有「非信徒」，又怎能標舉出「信徒」呢？

In your dealings with people, can you detect subtle feelings of either superiority or inferiority toward them? You are looking at the ego, which lives through comparison.

Envy is a by-product of the ego, which feels diminished if something good happens to someone else, or someone has more, knows more, or can do more than you. The ego's identity depends on comparison and feeds on *more*. It will grasp at anything. If all else fails, you can strengthen your fictitious sense of self through seeing yourself as *more* unfairly treated by life or *more* ill than someone else.

What are the stories, the fictions from which you derive your sense of self ?

$$\int$$

Built into the very structure of the egoic self is a need to oppose, resist, and exclude to maintain the sense of separateness on which its continued survival depends. So there is "me" against the "other," "us" against "them."

The ego needs to be in conflict with something or someone. That explains why you are looking for peace and joy and love but cannot tolerate them for very long. You say you want happiness but are addicted to your unhappiness.

　　與人相處時，你能察覺自己內在的微妙感受嗎？它可能是優越感或自卑感。你看見的正是「小我」，它藉由比較而生存。

　　妒忌是小我的副產品，如果某些好事降臨到別人身上，或是某人比你擁有更多、知道更多，或是能力更好時，小我便感覺自己被削弱了。小我是透過比較來建立自我的認同，並以比別人更多來壯大自己。它不斷地與任何東西、任何事情進行比較，如果都比輸了，便會藉認定自己遭受了更多不公平的對待，或比別人有更多的不幸，來強化那虛假的自我感。

　　你的自我感來自什麼樣的虛構的情節，它的故事內容究竟是什麼？

$$\int$$

　　小我本身有個十分明顯的特色，就是它需要去反對、抗拒、排外，以維持那人我有別的分離感，因為這感受，小我得以繼續生存。所以，是「我」在對抗「其他人」，是「我們」在對抗「他們」。

　　小我需要和某人、某事維持對立、衝突，這就解釋了為何你總在尋求平安、喜悅與愛，但又無法忍受它們太久。你說你想要快樂，卻又對你的不快樂上了癮。

Your unhappiness ultimately arises not from the circumstances of your life but from the conditioning of your mind.

∫

Do you carry feelings of guilt about something you did — or failed to do — in the past? This much is certain: you acted according to your level of consciousness or rather unconsciousness at that time. If you had been more aware, more conscious, you would have acted differently.

Guilt is another attempt by the ego to create an identity, a sense of self. To the ego, it doesn't matter whether that self is positive or negative. What you did or failed to do was a manifestation of unconsciousness — human unconsciousness. The ego, however, personalizes it and says, "I did that," and so you carry a mental image of yourself as "bad."

Throughout history humans have inflicted count- less violent, cruel, and hurtful acts on each other, and continue to do so. Are they all to be condemned; are they all guilty?

　　你的不快樂不是因為你的人生處境，而是因為你心智的制約反應。

$$\int$$

　　你是否對於自己過去曾經做過或沒能去做的某件事感到內疚？可以確定的是，你在做的當下，是依據當時內在意識的清醒程度，或甚至根本是無意識而這麼行事的。如果你當時更為覺察，更有意識，你的行事就會有所不同。

　　內疚是小我建立自我感與自我身分的另一種方式。對小我而言，自我是正面的抑或是負面的，根本不重要。你過去所做的或沒能做成的某件事，皆只是人類集體無意識*的外在顯化。然而，小我卻將它個人化說：「是我做的。」於是你就認為自己是「不好的」。

　　綜觀歷史，人類加諸彼此身上的暴虐、殘忍與傷害難以計數，而且還在持續進行中。這些人難道全都該遭受譴責？他們

＊人類集體無意識 human unconsciousness
艾克哈特認為，一個沒有覺知力的人，他的行為與舉止並不是他「選擇或決定」下的結果，而是受到「集體無意識」牽引下的產物；但是在表面上看起來，是這個人做了什麼事，而且這個人也認為這是他做的。事實上，這些都是小我所創造出來的幻覺。因此，艾克哈特認為，一個沒有覺知力的人，是無法也不能對自己的行為負責。更進一步說，人類集體如果也是受到慣性牽引，活在小我中，同樣也是無法為自己行為負責任的人類集體無意識。

Or are those acts simply expressions of unconsciousness, an evolutionary stage that we are now growing out of?

Jesus' words, "Forgive them for they know not what they do," also apply to yourself.

∫

If you set egoic goals for the purpose of freeing yourself, enhancing yourself or your sense of importance, even if you achieve them, they will not satisfy you.

Set goals, but know that the arriving is not all that important. When anything arises out of presence, it means this moment is not a means to an end: the doing is fulfilling in itself every moment. You are no longer reducing the Now to a means to an end, which is the egoic consciousness.

∫

"No self. No problem," said the Buddhist Master when asked to explain the deeper meaning of Buddhism.

全都有罪嗎？或者，這些行為僅只是無意識的表現，僅只是當今人類都必須成長經歷的一個進化階段？

耶穌說過：「天父啊！原諒他們，因為他們不知道自己在做什麼。」這句話同樣也適用於你自己身上。

假若你為了解放自己、強固自己或增加自己的重要性，而設定小我的目標，即使你達成了這樣的目標，它們終究無法使你得到滿足。

你可以設定目標，但要知道，達成目標並非那麼重要。於「臨在」中不論生起什麼，都說明著「此時此刻」不是前往目的地的工具而已——你的「做」已然在它自身得到滿足，你不會再矮化當下，把它當成達到目標的工具，只有小我才會這麼認為。

有人請問佛教大師關於佛教更深層的意義時，大師道：「無我，無問題。」

當下
The Now

4

On the surface it seems that the present moment is only one of many, many moments. Each day of your life appears to consist of thousands of moments where different things happen. Yet if you look more deeply, is there not only one moment, ever? Is life ever not "this moment"?

This one moment — Now — is the only thing you can never escape from, the one constant factor in your life. No matter what happens, no matter how much your life changes, one thing is certain: it's always Now.

Since there is no escape from the Now, why not welcome it, become friendly with it?

When you make friends with the present moment, you feel at home no matter where you are. When you don't feel at home in the Now, no matter where you go, you will carry unease with you.

　　表面看來，「此時此刻」似乎僅是眾多片刻中的一刻。你生命中的每一天看似由無數的片刻所構成，在其間許許多多不同的事情發生了，但如果你更深入來看，始終不是只有一個時刻嗎？生命中何時不是「此時此刻」呢？

　　此時此刻──當下，是你永遠無法逃脫的唯一一刻。它是你生命中一個恆常不變的元素。不論發生任何事，不論你的人生如何改變，有件事是不變的：你面對的永遠是當下。

　　既然無法從當下逃脫，為何不張開雙臂歡迎它，與它友善相處呢？

　　當你與當下為友，無論你身處何方，都會感覺像回家般自在。如果你在當下無法感受到這樣的自在，那無論你到哪裡，都不會感到心安。

The present moment is as it is. Always. Can you let it be?

The division of life into past, present, and future is mind-made and ultimately illusory. Past and future are thought forms, mental abstractions. The past can only be remembered Now. What you remember is an event that took place in the Now, and you remember it Now. The future, when it comes, is the Now. So the only thing that is real, the only thing there ever is the Now.

現前這一刻永遠都是如其所是，你能否順其自然呢？

　　將人生切割成過去、現在與未來是心智的把戲，而這最終還是虛幻不實的。過去與未來是思維意念，是心智上的抽象概念。過去只能在當下被憶起。你所記起的種種是在過去的當下*發生的事情，只是在現在這個當下你記起了它。而未來，當它來臨時，即是當下正在發生的事情。所以，唯一真實的，唯一真正存在的，即是當下正在發生的事情。

＊當下 the Now
艾克哈特對於「now」與「the Now」有細微的不同用法。全書中「now」，大部分是用作副詞「當下地」，以形容動詞；一小部分是作為形容詞「當下的」。但是，「the Now」變成了一個名詞「當下」，指的是現在正在發生的事情，當下正在發生的事情。中文在這些詞性上的分辨很模糊，所以，「What you remember is an event that took place in the Now」這句話，是指你所記起的種種是在過去的當下中發生的事情，是在現在這個當下你記起了它。在此要強調的是，未來與過去只是一個「心智上的概念」。

To have your attention in the Now is not a denial of what is needed in your life. It is recognizing what is primary. Then you can deal with what is secondary with great ease. It is not saying, "I'm not dealing with things anymore because there is only the Now." No. Find what is primary first, and make the Now into your friend, not your enemy. Acknowledge it, honor it. When the Now is the foundation and primary focus of your life, then your life unfolds with ease.

∫

Putting away the dishes, drawing up a business strategy, planning a trip — what is more important: the doing or the result that you want to achieve through the doing? This moment or some future moment?

Do you treat *this moment* as if it were an obstacle to be overcome? Do you feel you have a future moment to get to that is more important?

Almost everyone lives like this most of the time. Since the future never arrives, except *as* the present, it is a dysfunctional way to live. It generates a constant undercurrent of unease, tension, and discontent. It does not honor life, which is Now and never not Now.

專注於當下，並不是全盤否認生命所需求的事物，而是要你認清什麼是最重要的，然後在面對生命中次要的事物，便能怡然自得了。專注於當下，並非宣稱：「唯有當下，所以我將不再理會其他世事。」絕非如此。專注於當下是指專注於當下正在發生的種種，然後找出當下最需要關注與處理的事，並與當下結為盟友而非敵人，接納它、讚美它。一旦你的生命奠基於當下並聚焦其上，你的人生自然而然地就開展了。

∫

收拾碗盤、草擬商業策略、策劃旅行……，什麼比較重要呢？是手上正在做的事情？還是你透過做這些事想達到的結果？是此時此刻？還是未來的某個時刻？

你是否將「此時此刻」視為一個得去克服的障礙？你是否覺得有個更重要的未來你得奔赴？

幾乎每個人大半輩子都這樣活著，然而，未來永遠不會到來，除非臨至當下，所以如果一輩子這樣活著，豈不是無法良好運作嗎？活在未來會引發一股充滿不安、緊張與不滿的經常性暗流，這對生命並不尊重，因為生命就在當下，它從來沒有不在當下。

∫

Feel the aliveness within your body. That anchors you in the Now.

∫

Ultimately you are not taking responsibility for life until you take responsibility for *this moment* — Now. This is because Now is the only place where life can be found.

Taking responsibility for this moment means not to oppose internally the "suchness" of Now, not to argue with what is. It means to be in alignment with life.

The Now is as it is because it cannot be otherwise. What Buddhists have always known, physicists now confirm: there are no isolated things or events. Underneath the surface appearance, all things are interconnected, are part of the totality of the cosmos that has brought about the form that this moment takes.

When you say "yes" to what is, you become aligned with the power and intelligence of Life itself. Only then can you become an agent for positive change in the world.

感受內在的蓬勃生氣，將使你定錨於當下。

除非你對「此時此刻」負責，否則你終究無法對生命負責。這是因為當下是你唯一可以發現生命的地方。

對此時此刻負責，意味著內心不要抗拒當下的「如是」，也不要與實際的狀況爭辯，而要與生命結為盟友。

當下是什麼狀況就是什麼狀況，因為它不可能是其他狀況。佛弟子對此早有領悟，如今物理學家也一一證實：宇宙萬物間，沒有獨立存在的事或物。表相之下，萬事萬物互有關連，同屬宇宙整體的一部分，而正是從這宇宙裡緣生出此刻所顯現的所有形相。

當你對事情的實際狀況俯首稱「是」時，你將與本智及生命本身的力量結為盟友。唯有如此，世界才能透過你，朝向正面改變。

∫

A simple but radical spiritual practice is to accept whatever arises in the Now — within and without.

∫

When your attention moves into the Now, there is an alertness. It is as if you were waking up from a dream, the dream of thought, the dream of past and future. Such clarity, such simplicity. No room for problem-making. Just this moment as it is.

∫

The moment you enter the Now with your attention, you realize that life is sacred. There is a sacredness to everything you perceive when you are present. The more you live in the Now, the more you sense the simple yet profound joy of Being and the sacredness of all life.

∫

　　一種簡單但根本的靈修練習方法，就是從內到外全然接納當下所生起的一切。

∫

　　當你把專注力移轉到當下，警覺就會出現。就像從一場夢中醒來，一場思緒之夢，一場過去與未來的夢。它是如此地清晰，如此地單純，問題沒有可存身的空間，唯有此刻，如其本是。

∫

　　當你將專注帶入當下的那一刻，你將了解生命是神聖的。當你臨於當下，你所感知的一切都將是聖潔純淨的。你愈能活在當下，便愈能感受到單純卻深刻的「本體的喜悅」，以及所有生命的聖潔。

Most people confuse the Now with *what* happens in the
Now, but that's not what it is. The Now is deeper than what
happens in it. It is the space in which it happens.

So do not confuse the content of this moment with the
Now. The Now is deeper than any content that arises in it.

When you step into the Now, you step out of the content
of your mind. The incessant stream of thinking slows
down. Thoughts don't absorb all your attention anymore,
don't draw you in totally. Gaps arise in between thoughts —
spaciousness, stillness. You begin to realize how much vaster
and deeper you are than your thoughts.

大多數人們分不清「當下」與「在當下裡所發生的事情」，
此兩者並不相同。「當下」是事情發生的空間，它要比其中「發
生的事情」更深、更廣。

　　所以，不要將「此刻發生了什麼」與「當下」有所混淆，
「當下」要比在其中發生的任何內容都更深、更廣。

　　當你進入了當下，你便跨出了心智世界，奔流不息的思維
之流慢了下來。念頭不再佔據你全部的注意，不再全然地吸
引著你。念頭與念頭之間的空隙出現了──無垠寬廣、寂然靜
止。你開始了解──你，遠比你的思維更為浩瀚與深刻。

Thoughts, emotions, sense perceptions, and what- ever you experience make up the content of your life. "My life" is what you derive your sense of self from, and "my life" is content, or so you believe.

You continuously overlook the most obvious fact: your innermost sense of I *Am* has nothing to do with what *happens* in your life, nothing to do with content. That sense of *I Am* is one with the Now. It always remains the same. In childhood and old age, in health or sickness, in success or failure, the *I Am* — the space of Now — remains unchanged at its deepest level. It usually gets confused with content, and so you experience *I Am* or the Now only faintly and indirectly, *through* the content of your life. In other words: your sense of Being becomes obscured by circumstances, your stream of thinking, and the many things of this world. The Now becomes obscured by time.

And so you forget your rootedness in Being, your divine reality, and lose yourself in the world. Confusion, anger, depression, violence, and conflict arise when humans forget who they are.

　　思維、情緒、感官覺受，以及任何你所經歷體驗的，構成了你的生命的內容。「我的生命」是自我感的來源，而你所謂的「我的生命」就是生活中的這些內容，或者你相信是如此。

　　你一直忽略一件顯而易見的事實：你內心深處的「我本是」，與你生命中所「發生」的事情，與你所謂的生命內容，絲毫無關。「我本是」與當下是合一的，它始終不變，幼年如此，老年亦然，無論健康或生病、成功或失敗，「我本是」——當下的覺性空間*，在最深層的意義上，它從來沒改變過。人們常以為生命的內容就是「我本是」，而透過生命的內容，你也只能隱約、間接地體驗到「我本是」或「當下」。換句話說：你的本體感因為受到如思維之流或俗事等各種情況的遮蔽，而變得朦朧不清。「當下」也因為有了過去與未來的時間概念，而變得隱晦不明。

　　因此，你遺忘了你是根植於本體的，遺忘了你原有的神性，以致在這人世間迷失了自己。當人們遺忘了自己是誰，混亂、憤怒、沮喪、暴力與衝突便應運而生。

---

*當下的覺性空間 the space of Now
在此，艾克哈特是將覺性比擬為能感知萬事萬物的背景空間，亦即在覺性當中，萬事萬物被感知到；也可以說在覺性的空間裡，萬事萬物發生在其中。艾克哈特也在第一章時，以「內在空間」(inner space) 來指稱覺性。

Yet how easy it is to remember the truth and thus return home: I am not my thoughts, emotions, sense perceptions, and experiences. I am not the content of my life. I am Life. I am the space in which all things happen. I am consciousness. I am the Now. I Am.

然而，憶起真理，回歸本性是多麼容易：

我不是我的想法、情緒、感覺或種種經驗，

我也不是我的生命內容，我就是生命。

我就是萬事萬物發生的所在空間，

我就是那意識，

我就是當下，我本是。

誰是
真正的你？

Who You Truly Are

The Now is inseparable from who you are at the deepest level.

∫

Many things in your life matter, but only one thing matters absolutely.

It matters whether you succeed or fail in the eyes of the world. It matters whether you are healthy or not healthy, whether you are educated or not educated. It matters whether you are rich or poor — it certainly makes a difference in your life. Yes, all these things matter, relatively speaking, but they don't matter absolutely.

There is something that matters more than any of those things and that is finding the essence of who you are beyond that short-lived entity, that short-lived personalized sense of self.

You find peace not by rearranging the circumstances of your life, but by realizing who you are at the deepest level.

∫

當下，與最深層的「你」是密不可分的。

在你生命中有許多事情很重要，但只有一件事是絕對重要的。

在世俗眼光中，成功或失敗，這很重要；身體健不健康，是否接受了教育，這也很重要；有錢或沒錢，這當然更重要，它肯定讓你生命有所差別。這一切都是要緊的，但也只是從相對上來看；放到絕對上說時，它們都不是至關緊要的了。

有件事要比這其中的任何一件都重要，那就是能超越有限的肉體生命與個人自我意識，而找到究竟的你。

你無法靠重新安排人生的處境來覓得內在的平安，你得透過認識內心最深處「你究竟是誰」來找到它。

Reincarnation doesn't help you if in your next incarnation you still don't know who you are.

∫

All the misery on the planet arises due to a personalized sense of "me" or "us". That covers up the essence of who you are. When you are unaware of that inner essence, in the end you always create misery. It's as simple as that. When you don't know who you are, you create a mind-made self as a substitute for your beautiful divine being and cling to that fearful and needy self.

Protecting and enhancing that false sense of self then becomes your primary motivating force.

∫

Many expressions that are in common usage, and sometimes the structure of language itself, reveal the fact that people don't know who they are. You say: "He lost his life" or "my life," as if life were something that you can possess or lose. The truth is: you don't *have* a life, you *are*

　　倘若來世你依然不明白你是誰，那麼即使輪迴轉世也幫不
了你了。

　　地球上所有的苦難，皆源於「我」或「我們」這樣的個人
分別意識，它掩蓋了你的究竟本質。當你未能覺察自己內在的
本質時，你就會一直製造痛苦，事情就這麼簡單。當你不知道
自己是誰，你就會創造出一個由心智所打造的自我，取代你那
完美的神性本體，而且還緊抓住那滿懷恐懼與匱乏的自我不願
鬆手。

　　於是保護並鞏固那虛假的自我意識，就成為你生命中最主
要的動力。

　　人們不知道「自己到底是誰」這個事實，可以從許多生活
習慣用語的表達，以及某些語言本身的結構上看出來。當你
說：「他失去了他的生命」或「我的生命」，就像在說，生命是

life. The One Life, the one consciousness that pervades the entire universe and takes temporary form to experience itself as a stone or a blade of grass, as an animal, a person, a star or a galaxy.

Can you sense deep within that you already know that? Can you sense that you already are That?

∫

For most things in life, you need time: to learn a new skill, build a house, become an expert, make a cup of tea... Time is useless, however, for the most essential thing in life, the one thing that really matters : self-realization, which means knowing who you are beyond the surface self — beyond your name, your physical form, your history, your story.

You cannot find yourself in the past or future. The only place where you can find yourself is in the Now.

Spiritual seekers look for self-realization or enlightenment in the future. To be a seeker implies that you need the future. If this is what you believe, it becomes true for you: you *will* need time until you realize that you don't need time to be who you are.

某種你可以擁有或失去的東西。但真相是：你並不是擁有生命，你就是生命本身。這個宇宙共同生命或宇宙共同意識，瀰漫於天地之間，並以某個暫時的外在形相來體驗生命本身，那形相或許是一顆石頭、一片草葉、一隻動物、一個人、一顆星星，甚至一個星系。

在內心深處，你是否能感到其實你是明白這件事的？你能感到自己其實就是那宇宙共同生命的本身？

$$\int$$

生命中大多數的事物，都需要時間，如學習新技術、蓋棟房子、成為某種專家、泡杯茶等。然而，時間對於生命中最本質的事，那唯一重要的事——自我了悟，卻是毫無意義的。自我了悟是指超越表面的自我——你的名字、你的肉體、你的個人歷史與故事，而去認識自己到底是誰。

你無法在過去或未來裡找到自己。唯一可以找到你自己的地方，就在當下。

靈性追求者追求醒覺或自我了悟於未來。既為追求者，便意味著需要未來，如果這就是你所相信的，它對你而言就是真的：因為你將會需要時間，直到你真正明白做自己並不需要時間。

When you look at a tree, you are aware of the tree. When you have a thought or feeling, you are aware of that thought or feeling. When you have a pleasurable or painful experience, you are aware of that experience.

These seem to be true and obvious statements, yet if you look at them very closely, you will find that in a subtle way their very structure contains a fundamental illusion, an illusion that is unavoidable when you use language. Thought and language create an apparent duality and a separate person where there is none. The truth is: you are not somebody who is aware of the tree, the thought, feeling, or experience. You are the awareness or consciousness in and by which those things appear.

As you go about your life, can you be aware of yourself as the awareness in which the entire content of your life unfolds?

當你凝視一棵樹，你覺察那棵樹；當你有個念頭或感覺閃過，你覺察那念頭或感覺；當你體驗愉快或痛苦，你覺察那體驗。

　　這些說法似乎真實且明顯，但如果你仔細檢視將會發現，這些說法的結構中很隱微地包含了一個基本的錯覺，一個當你使用語言時很難避免的錯覺，那就是思考與語言創造了一個表相的二元世界，以及一個實際上並不存在的個人。真相是：並沒有一個「你」覺察到樹、念頭、感覺或體驗，你就是那覺察或意識，事物在意識之中生起，並透過意識顯現出來。

　　當你忙於你的人生，你能否覺察到你自己就是這個覺性，你人生的種種皆在這當中展現？

You say, "I want to know myself." You *are* the "I." You *are* the knowing. You *are* the consciousness through which everything is known. And that cannot *know* itself; it *is* itself.

There is nothing to know beyond that, and yet all knowing arises out of it. The "I" cannot make itself into an object of knowledge, of consciousness.

So you cannot become an object to yourself. That is the very reason the illusion of egoic identity arose — because mentally you made yourself into an object. "That's me," you say. And then you begin to have a relationship with yourself, and tell others and yourself your story.

By knowing yourself as the awareness in which phenomenal existence happens, you become free of dependency on phenomena and free of self-seeking in situations, places, and conditions. In other words: what happens or doesn't happen is not that important anymore. Things lose their heaviness, their seriousness. A playfulness comes into your life. You recognize this world as a cosmic dance, the dance of form — no more and no less.

你說：「我想知道我是誰。」其實，你就是這個能知道的「我」，你就是那個「了知」，你就是那個覺知的意識，因為有它，萬事萬物才可以被察覺。而覺知是無法覺知到自己的，因為它本身就是覺知。

除了了解到你就是覺知本身之外，就再也沒有什麼需要了解的了；而所有你所了解到的，都是由這個覺知中生起。這個能覺知的「我」，無法將它自己變成一個被知道或被覺知的對象。

所以，你不可能成為被自己所覺知的一個對象。只要你在心智上將自己當成一個可以被覺知的對象，「小我認同」的錯覺便會生起。當你說：「那就是我。」你就開始與自己產生一種相對關係，並告訴他人和（錯覺所生的）「你自己」關於你的故事。

∫

只要明白你自己就是那個覺知，明白所有現象的存在都是在這覺知裡發生的，你就從對現象的依賴中解脫了，你不再於不同的處境、不同的地點與不同的狀況中尋找自我。換句話說，發生了什麼，或者什麼也沒發生，都不再重要了。世間的一切都不再沉重、嚴肅，活潑與開心進到你的生活裡，世界在你的認知中就像一齣宇宙之舞，一齣表相之舞——不多也不少，恰如其是。

∫

When you know who you truly are, there is an abiding alive sense of peace. You could call it joy because that's what joy is: vibrantly alive peace. It is the joy of knowing yourself as the very life essence before life takes on form. That is the joy of Being — of being who you truly are.

∫

Just as water can be solid, liquid, or gaseous, consciousness can be seen to be "frozen" as physical matter, "liquid" as mind and thought, or formless as pure consciousness.

Pure consciousness is Life before it comes into manifestation, and that Life looks at the world of form through "your" eyes because consciousness is who you are. When you know yourself as That, then you recognize yourself in everything. It is a state of complete clarity of perception. You are no longer an entity with a heavy past that becomes a screen of concepts through which every experience is interpreted.

∫

　　當你認識到真正的自己時，你會有一種持續的、活生生的平靜感。你可以稱之為「喜悅」，因為喜悅就是充滿生氣的平靜。這個喜悅是來自於，你認識到了自己正是那個尚未披上形相的外衣，無形無相的生命本質。這是本體的喜悅──是做真正的自己的喜悅。

∫

　　正如水有固態、液態、氣態三態，意識也可以被理解為有三種類似的狀態：如固態凝固的物質、如液態流動的意念，以及如氣態無形的純粹意識。

　　純粹意識是生命尚未顯化為形相之前的狀態。因為你就是那個能覺知的意識，生命透過你的雙眼，才會看到這有形的世界。當你知道自己就是那個能覺知的意識，你就可以於萬事萬物中認出你自己。這是一種全然澄澈明白的知覺狀態。你不再是個揹著沉重過去的實體，那沉重的過去形成一種觀念上的遮屏，你透過這個遮屏去詮釋所有的經驗。

When you perceive without interpretation, you can then sense what it is that is perceiving. The most we can say in language is that there is a field of alert stillness in which the perception happens.

Through "you", formless consciousness has become aware of itself.

∫

Most people's lives are run by desire and fear.

Desire is the need to *add* something to yourself in order to *be* yourself more fully. All fear is the fear of *losing* something and thereby becoming diminished and *being* less.

These two movements obscure the fact that Being cannot be given or taken away. Being in its fullness is already within you, Now.

當你知道自己就是那個能覺知的意識，你就可以在萬事萬物中認出自己。當你不帶詮釋地去感知一切時，你就可以如實地覺察到感知對象的本來面貌，用語言的極限來形容，那就是鮮活的靜觀寂照之境，感官知覺就是從這裡面生起的。

透過「你」，無形無相的意識覺察到它自己。

大多數人的生命被欲望與恐懼所掌控。

欲望，是想給自己增添些什麼，好讓自己更為完滿。恐懼則是害怕自己失去什麼，因為減損而變得更少。

這兩者都模糊了一個事實—本體是不能夠增或減的。就在當下，本體存在的圓滿你已完全俱足。

接納與臣服
Acceptance & Surrender

6

Whenever you are able, have a "look" inside yourself to see whether you are unconsciously creating conflict between the inner and the outer, between your external circumstances at that moment — where you are, who you are with, or what you are doing — and your thoughts and feelings. Can you feel how painful it is to internally stand in opposition to what *is* ?

When you recognize this, you also realize that you are now free to give up this futile conflict, this inner state of war.

∫

How often each day, if you were to verbalize your inner reality at that moment, would you have to say, "I don't want to be where I am?" What does it feel like when you don't want to be where you are — the traffic jam, your place of work, the airport lounge, the people you are with?

It is true, of course, that some places are good places to walk out of — and sometimes that may well be the most appropriate thing for you to do. In many cases, however, walking out is not an option. In all those cases, the "I don't want to be here" is not only useless but also dysfunctional. It makes you and others unhappy.

　　只要你可以，請記得隨時往自己內心「看」一眼，看看自己是不是於無意識間，又在製造內與外的衝突——你讓內心種種想法、感覺，與當時外在的情況（你在哪裡、你與誰在一起、你正在做什麼）起衝突；你可以感覺到當你與如是對抗時，是多麼痛苦嗎？

　　一旦你認知到這痛苦時，你同時也會明白，你可以自由地放下這徒然無益的衝突，放下這內在的戰爭。

　　如果讓你把內心真實的感受用話語說出來，那麼在一天當中，將有多少次你會說：「我不想待在這裡？」不想待在自己當下置身之處（車陣之中、工作場所、候機室，不想與身旁的人共處），是什麼樣的感覺呢？

　　的確，有些地方直接離開是可以的，而且那樣做可能也是最適當的。然而，更多的時候，離開不見得是你可以選擇的，這時候，說出「我不想待在這裡」的念頭不僅毫無用處，更形成困擾，徒然使你與其他人都不快樂而已。

It has been said: wherever you go, there you are. In other words: you are here. Always. Is it so hard to accept that?

∫

Do you really need to mentally label every sense perception and experience? Do you really need to have a reactive like/dislike relationship with life where you are in almost continuous conflict with situations and people? Or is that just a deep-seated mental habit that can be broken? Not by doing anything, but by allowing this moment to be as it is.

∫

The habitual and reactive "no" strengthens the ego. "Yes" weakens it. Your form identity, the ego, cannot survive surrender.

　　俗話說：「既來之，則安之。」也就是說，永遠要「身在哪裡，心就在哪裡」。這很難以接受嗎？

$$\int$$

　　你非得在腦海中為每個感受與經驗貼標籤嗎？對你那不斷有人際或處境衝突的生命，你非得與它保持這種喜歡／不喜歡的互動關係嗎？也許，這根深柢固的習性是可以破除的，而且你不需要特別做什麼，只要如實地接納此時此刻的一切就行了。

$$\int$$

　　要強化小我，只需要慣性地回應：「不」；反之，回應「是」則可以弱化它。臣服之後，你的表相認同*—小我，是無法活存的。

＊表相認同 form identity
這裡的 form identity 指的是你怎麼看待自己，就是你對你的身體、情緒、念頭、反應等認同，以為它們就是自己。艾克哈特將所有的情緒、念頭、反應都稱為「form」，雖然嚴格說來，它們並無物理的形相。但是為什麼艾克哈特會稱它們為「form」？因為這些都是你的「意識」所能感知到的「對象」。你將你所感知到的對象安上一個標籤，認為那就是自己，但是，因為你是「覺知」本身，所以不能覺知到「覺知」。

∫

"I have so much to do." Yes, but what is the quality of your doing? Driving to work, speaking to clients, working on the computer, running errands, dealing with the countless things that make up your daily life — how total are you in what you do? Is your doing surrendered or non-surrendered? This is what determines your success in life, not how much effort you make. Effort implies stress and strain, *needing* to reach a certain point in the future or accomplish a certain result.

Can you detect even the slightest element within yourself of *not wanting* to be doing what you are doing? That is a denial of life, and so a truly successful outcome is not possible.

If you can detect this within yourself, can you also drop it and be total in what you do?

∫

"Doing one thing at a time" is how one Zen Master defined the essence of Zen.

∫

「我有好多事要做。」是的，但你做事的品質如何呢？當你開車去上班，或與客戶談話，或在電腦前工作，或跑腿打雜，處理多如牛毛的日常事務時，你全心投入了嗎？你是心不甘、情不願地去做？還是臣服地去做？決定人生成功與否的是臣服，而不是你付出多少努力。努力意味著壓力與緊張，意味著必須在未來達到一定的程度，或是完成一定的成果。

你可以覺察到自己並不想做手上的事嗎？即使只是絲毫的不願意。這可是對生命的一種否定，若真是如此，想真正成功是不可能的。

如果你可以偵知自己內在的這個不情願，你願意丟棄它，轉而全心投入你正在做的事情裡嗎？

∫

一位禪師如此定義「禪」：「一次只做一件事。」

Doing one thing at a time means to be total in what you do, to give it your complete attention. This is surrendered action — empowered action.

∫

Your acceptance of what *is* takes you to a deeper level where your inner state as well as your sense of self no longer depend on the mind's judgments of "good" or "bad."

When you say "yes" to the "isness" of life, when you accept this moment as it is, you can feel a sense of spaciousness within you that is deeply peaceful.

On the surface, you may still be happy when it's sunny and not so happy when it's rainy; you may be happy at winning a million dollars and unhappy at losing all your possessions. Neither happiness nor unhappiness, however, go all that deep anymore. They are ripples on the surface of your Being. The background peace within you remains undisturbed regardless of the nature of the outside condition.

The "yes" to what is reveals a dimension of depth within you that is dependent neither on external conditions nor on the internal conditions of constantly fluctuating thoughts and emotions.

「一次只做一件事」意味著用上全部的心力，全然地投入所做的事情，這是臣服的行為，是能強化力量的行為。

∫

如實地接受一切，將帶你進入一個更深刻的層次，在那裡，你的內在狀態與你的自我意識，將不再依賴心智所做出的好、壞判斷。

當你對生命的本然樣貌伏首稱「是」，當你依實際狀況全然地接納了此刻的一切，你將在心底感到無垠而深沉的平靜。

表面上，你還是會為天晴而開心，為陰雨而悶悶不樂；你也會在贏得百萬元時歡欣，在輸光一切後難過。然而，無論快樂或不快樂，它們都不會太深，它們只是生命本體表層掀動的漣漪。不論外在情境如何起伏，你內在如背景般的那片平安依然文風不動。

臣服於「事情的真實狀況」，將揭開你內在的一個深層境界：一個既不依賴外在情況，也不依賴內在念頭與情緒運作的世界。

∫

Surrender becomes so much easier when you realize the fleeting nature of all experiences and that the world cannot give you anything of lasting value. You then continue to meet people, to be involved in experiences and activities, but without the wants and fears of the egoic self. That is to say, you no longer demand that a situation, person, place, or event should satisfy you or make you happy. Its passing and imperfect nature is allowed to be.

And the miracle is that when you are no longer placing an impossible demand on it, every situation, person, place, or event becomes not only satisfying but also more harmonious, more peaceful.

∫

When you completely accept this moment, when you no longer argue with what *is* , the compulsion to think lessens and is replaced by an alert stillness. You are fully conscious, yet the mind is not labeling this moment in any way. This state of inner nonresistance opens you to the unconditioned

∫

　　當你明白所有的經驗本質上都是變動不居的，明白這世界無法給你恆定的價值時，臣服就變得容易多了。臣服之後，你依然與人們互動，依然參與各種體驗與活動，卻不再帶著小我諸多的欲望與恐懼。也就是說，你不再要求某個情境、某個人、某個地方或某事件，要讓你滿意或快樂。你接納了事物短暫與不完美的本質。

　　當你不再對生活提出不可能的要求時，奇蹟發生了，每個情境、每個人，甚至每件事不但都讓你滿意，同時彼此間也更和諧、更平靜。

∫

　　當你全然接納此刻，不再與事實本然抗拒，思考的衝動就會減低，取而代之的是一種鮮活的靜觀寂照。你的意識全然清晰，然而你的心智卻沒有對此時此刻貼上任何的標籤。這種內在不再抗拒的狀態，將引你進入不受制約的意識，那意識遠比

consciousness that is infinitely greater than the human mind. This vast intelligence can then express itself through you and assist you, both from within and from without. That is why, by letting go of inner resistance, you often find circumstances change for the better.

∫

Am I saying, "Enjoy this moment. Be happy?" No. Allow the "suchness" of this moment. That's enough.

∫

Surrender is surrender to *this moment* , not to a story through which you *interpret* this moment and then try to resign yourself to it.

For instance, you may have a disability and can't walk anymore. The condition is as it is.

Perhaps your mind is now creating a story that says, "This is what my life has come to. I have ended up in a wheelchair. Life has treated me harshly and unfairly. I don't deserve this."

人類心智更加浩瀚無垠。這浩瀚的本智,將透過你表現它自己,並由內到外幫助你。這就是為什麼當你放下了內心的抗拒,你常發現一切變得更美好了。

∫

我有說:「快樂地享受此時此刻」嗎?沒有。

接納此時此刻「如其所是」,便已足夠。

∫

臣服是指臣服於此時此刻,而非臣服於那個用來詮釋此刻,然後試著把自己交託給它的故事。

譬如,你身有殘障,再也無法行走。實況就是如此。

而你的心智卻在織造一個故事:「人生到此,我將在輪椅上終老一生。生命對我如此嚴酷不公,我不該遭到如此待遇。」

Can you accept the *isness* of this moment and not confuse it with a story the mind has created around it?

∫

Surrender comes when you no longer ask, "Why is this happening to me?"

∫

Even within the seemingly most unacceptable and painful situation is concealed a deeper good, and within every disaster is contained the seed of grace.

Throughout history, there have been women and men who, in the face of great loss, illness, imprisonment, or impending death, accepted the seemingly unacceptable and thus found "the peace that passeth all understanding."

Acceptance of the unacceptable is the greatest source of grace in this world.

∫

你能如實地接納此時此刻，不把它與心智圍繞著它所編織的故事混為一談嗎？

當你不再問：「為什麼這事發生在我身上？」你，便臣服了。

即使是看起來最難以接受以及最痛苦的惡境，也隱藏了一個更深層的善，而在每個災難的背後，也都包含了恩典的種籽。

在歷史上，很多男人或女人在面對巨大的損失、病痛、拘禁或即將臨至的死亡之際，他們選擇接受那看似難以接受的事實，進而找到那「不可思議的平安」。

接受那難以接受的，就是世上恩典的偉大源頭。

There are situations where all answers and explanations fail. Life does not make sense anymore. Or someone in distress comes to you for help, and you don't know what to do or say.

When you fully accept that you don't know, you give up struggling to find answers with the limited thinking mind, and that is when a greater intelligence can operate through you. And even thought can then benefit from that, since the greater intelligence can flow into it and inspire it.

Sometimes surrender means giving up trying to understand and becoming comfortable with not knowing.

∫

Do you know of someone whose main function in life seems to be to make themselves and others miserable, to spread unhappiness? Forgive them, for they too are part of the awakening of humanity. The role they play represents an intensification of the nightmare of egoic consciousness, the state of non-surrender. There is nothing personal in all this. It is not who they are.

∫

　　有那麼些時候，所有的答案與解釋都失靈了，生命變得沒什麼道理。某個煩惱憂傷的人前來求助，而你卻不知該說些什麼或做些什麼。

　　全然接納你自己的「不知道」，不再用力地以有限的思考去尋找答案，此時，一個更宏大的本智，將透過你開始運作。即使是你的思維也能從中受益，因為這更為宏大的本智，會注入思考中，給它啟發。

　　有時，「臣服」意味著「不再嘗試去理解」，而面對「不知道」也能處之泰然。

　　你認識那種一生就只會為自己和別人帶來不幸、散播不愉快的人嗎？請原諒他們吧！因為他們也是人類覺醒的部分。他們所扮演的角色，代表著強化的小我意識夢魘，是拒絕臣服的必然狀態。這一切非關個人，因為那不是他們真正的本質。

Surrender, one could say, is the inner transition from resistance to acceptance, from "no" to "yes." When you surrender, your sense of self shifts from being identified with a reaction or mental judgment to being the *space around* the reaction or judgment. It is a shift from identification with form — the thought or the emotion — to being and recognizing yourself as that which has no form — spacious awareness.

∫

Whatever you accept completely will take you to peace, including the acceptance that you cannot accept, that you are in resistance.

∫

Leave Life alone. Let it be.

　　「臣服」是從抗拒到接納，從「不」到「是」的一種內在轉化。當你臣服了，你的自我感將從認同於判斷分別與反應的狀態中，轉換成為包覆著這些分別與批判的「空間」。這是從認同於形相（念頭與情緒），轉化到認出自己就是那無形的廣袤覺知本身。

$$\int$$

　　任何你所對抗的、難以接受的，一旦被你全然接納，都將引領你進入平靜。

$$\int$$

　　別去干擾生命，順其自然吧！

自然

Nature

7

We depend on nature not only for our physical survival. We also need nature to show us the way home, the way out of the prison of our own minds. We got lost in doing, thinking, remembering, anticipating — lost in a maze of complexity and a world of problems.

We have forgotten what rocks, plants, and animals still know. We have forgotten how to *be* — to be still, to be ourselves, to be where life is: Here and Now.

∫

Whenever you bring your attention to anything natural, anything that has come into existence without human intervention, you step out of the prison of conceptualized thinking and, to some extent, participate in the state of connectedness with Being in which everything natural still exists.

To bring your attention to a stone, a tree, or an animal does not mean to *think* about it, but simply to perceive it, to hold it in your awareness.

　　我們依賴自然，不僅是為了肉體活存的需要，也是為了讓它指引我們走出心智囚籠，回歸本性。我們迷失在不停地做、不停地想、不停地記存、不停地期待之中，我們迷失在一個錯綜複雜的迷宮和問題重重的世界之中。

　　我們遺忘了那些岩石、植物、動物都還知道的事。我們忘了如何安住——如何寂靜下來，如何做自己，如何回歸生命的本質——就在此地與當下。

$$\int$$

　　每當你把注意力放在任何自然的、非人為造作的事物上時，你就跨出了概念化思考的牢籠；從某種程度來說，你已與依舊存在於這些事物中的生命本質相連接了。

　　把注意力放在一顆石頭、一株大樹，或一隻動物，並不意味著去「思考」它，而是單純地去感受它，把它納入自己的覺性裡。

Something of its essence then transmits itself to you. You can sense how still it is, and in doing so the same stillness arises within you. You sense how deeply it rests in Being — completely at one with what it is and where it is. In realizing this, you too come to a place of rest deep within yourself.

When walking or resting in nature, honor that realm by being there fully. Be still. Look. Listen. See how every animal and every plant is completely itself. Unlike humans, they have not split themselves in two. They do not live through mental images of themselves, so they do not need to be concerned with trying to protect and enhance those images. The deer *is* itself. The daffodil *is* itself.

All things in nature are not only one with themselves but also one with the totality. They haven't removed themselves from the fabric of the whole by claiming a separate existence: "me" and the rest of the universe.

The contemplation of nature can free you of that "me," the great troublemaker.

　　接著，它本質裡的什麼就將它自己傳遞給你，你將感受到它是如此地寂靜，於是，你的內在也將生起同樣的寂靜。你感受到它是如此深沉地安住於本體之中，完全與它自己，與它所在的地方合而為一。明白這一切，你回到自心深處，安住在那裡。

　　在大自然中行走或休息時，以完全融入來禮讚這塊大地吧！寂靜下來，去看、去聽。看看每隻動物和每株植物如何全然是它自己，它們和人類不同，沒有將自己一分為二，也不仰賴自己塑造的心理形象而活。所以，它們不需要費心去保護與鞏固這些形象。鹿就是鹿，黃水仙花就是黃水仙花。

　　自然界的萬物，不只與自己合而為一，同時也與全體合而為一。它們並未將自己從共生的整體中抽離開來，而宣告宇宙中有「我」這個獨立個體的存在，以相對於宇宙中其他的存在。

　　寂靜下來，沉思自然，將使你從那個「我」，那個製造麻煩的高手之中解脫出來。

Bring awareness to the many subtle sounds of nature — the rustling of leaves in the wind, rain- drops falling, the humming of an insect, the first birdsong at dawn. Give yourself completely to the act of listening. Beyond the sounds there is something greater: a sacredness that cannot be under stood through thought.

∫

You didn't create your body, nor are you able to control the body's functions. An intelligence greater than the human mind is at work. It is the same intelligence that sustains all of nature. You cannot get any closer to that intelligence than by being aware of your own inner energy field — by feeling the aliveness, the animating presence within the body.

∫

The playfulness and joy of a dog, its unconditional love and readiness to celebrate life at any moment often contrast sharply with the inner state of the dog's owner — depressed, anxious, burdened by problems, lost in thought, not present

　　把覺察帶到自然裡那些細微的聲音上——樹葉在風中颯颯作響、滴落的雨聲、昆蟲嗡嗡哼唱、拂曉時第一聲鳥鳴。凝神去傾聽，超越那些聲音之後，有個更偉大的存在：一種無法以思考去理解的神聖。

　　你的身體不是你創造的，你也無法控制身體的各種功能，那都是由一個遠比人類心智更大的本智所運作的，這本智也育養著自然界的一切。你無法接近這本智，除非你察覺自己內在的能量場，也就是去感受體內那蓬勃的生氣，以及那生意盎然的「臨在」。

　　狗兒嬉鬧玩耍，充滿喜悅，牠們對愛毫無保留，並隨時準備歡慶生命。而狗主人卻經常是沮喪、焦慮、肩負著種種的問題、迷失在思慮中，更無法「臨在」於此地、此刻。狗與主人

in the only place and only time there is: Here and Now. One wonders: living with this person, how does the dog manage to remain so sane, so joyous?

When you perceive nature only through the mind, through thinking, you cannot sense its aliveness, its beingness. You see the form only and are unaware of the life within the form — the sacred mystery. Thought reduces nature to a commodity to be used in the pursuit of profit or knowledge or some other utilitarian purpose. The ancient forest becomes timber, the bird a research project, the mountain something to be mined or conquered.

When you perceive nature, let there be spaces of no thought, no mind. When you approach nature in this way, it will respond to you and participate in the evolution of human and planetary consciousness.

Notice how present a flower is, how surrendered to life.

彼此鮮明的對比，讓人不禁想問：狗兒與這樣的主人相處，是
怎麼把自己保持得這麼正常、這麼喜悅呢？

　　若你只是透過心智，透過思考來感受自然，你將無法感受
到它的蓬勃生機、它律動的生命。你只看見外在形體，卻察覺
不到表相之內的生命——那神聖的奧妙。思考將自然貶抑為只
是用來追求利潤、知識或其他功利目的的商品，例如：古老的
森林變成了木材，鳥類變成了研究項目，山岳變成了要被開採
或被征服的地方。

　　感受自然時，你得讓你的內心成為沒有念頭、沒有思考的
空間。當你以這樣的方式接近自然，它將回應你，並且開始參
與人類與地球意識的進化。

　　去觀察一朵花如何「臨在」於當下，如何臣服於生命。

∫

The plant that you have in your home — have you ever truly looked at it? Have you allowed that familiar yet mysterious being we call *plant* to teach you its secrets ? Have you noticed how deeply peaceful it is? How it is surrounded by a field of stillness? The moment you become aware of a plant's emanation of stillness and peace, that plant becomes your teacher.

∫

Watch an animal, a flower, a tree, and see how it rests in Being. It *is* itself. It has enormous dignity, innocence, and holiness. However, for you to see that, you need to go beyond the mental habit of naming and labeling. The moment you look beyond mental labels, you feel that ineffable dimension of nature that cannot be understood by thought or perceived through the senses. It is a harmony, a sacredness that permeates not only the whole of nature but is also within you.

ʃ

　　你曾經認真地觀察過自己家中的植物嗎？你曾經允許那熟悉卻又神祕，被我們稱為「植物」的生命體來教導你它的祕密嗎？你是否注意到它是多麼地深穩平靜？是如何地被籠罩在一片寂照之中？當你能覺察到一株植物所散發的寂照與平靜，那一刻，這株植物就是你的導師了。

ʃ

　　凝視一隻動物、一朵花、一棵樹，觀看它如何安住於本體之中。它就是它自己，擁有極大的莊嚴、純真與神聖。然而，若你想看到這一切，就必須超越為自然命名與歸類的心理習慣，當你跨越貼標籤式的觀看，那一刻，你將感受到自然裡一種難以名狀的層面，那層面無法透過思考去了解，也無法通過感官去感受，它是一種和諧，一種不僅瀰漫於整個自然之中，同時也充滿於你內在的神聖。

∫

The air that you breathe is nature, as is the breathing process itself.

Bring your attention to your breathing and realize that you are not doing it. It is the breath of nature. If you had to remember to breathe, you would soon die, and if you tried to stop breathing, nature would prevail.

You reconnect with nature in the most intimate and powerful way by becoming aware of your breathing and learning to hold your attention there. This is a healing and deeply empowering thing to do. It brings about a shift in consciousness from the conceptual world of thought to the inner realm of unconditioned consciousness.

∫

你呼吸的空氣是自然，而呼吸的進行本身也是自然。

把你的注意力帶到你的呼吸上，你就會了解，不是你在呼吸，是大自然在呼吸。如果得經由提醒你才記得呼吸，那你很快就會死亡；然而，如果你試著停止呼吸，自然可不會讓你得逞，它將取得最後的勝利。

去覺察你的呼吸並專注其上，是與自然重新產生連結最親密、最有力的方法，它也是一件既具有療癒功能又可強力加持的事。它帶來了意識的轉換*，從思維的概念化國度，轉移到內在「不受制約意識」之境。

---

*意識的轉換 a shift in consciousness
這裡要回顧意識的三態──如固態凝固的物質，如液態流動的意念，以及如氣態無形的純粹意識。其實，我們都是同時地在經驗著這三態。例如，看著一朵花，花本身是意識的固態，我們透過心智生起了「這是花」的念頭（意識的液態）；然後，我們的意識覺察到了這個念頭，這個「能覺察到念頭」的覺性是意識的氣態。但情況往往是，當念頭一生起時，「這是花」的念頭便擄獲我們的注意力，我們會認為這個意念中的「花」以及牽連出關於花的種種知識、好惡才是真的，反而不那麼「在覺察」這朵真正的花了。所以，這裡的「shift」是要能從過度地去認同思維念頭（即透過思維概念頭去「看」花，屬於意識的液態），轉換成為直接透過純粹意識去體驗這朵花，這樣你才能看到「真正的花」，而不是看到「經過思維折射過的花」。這個轉換的動作只是把你原來對思維的認同（專注），轉換成為對純粹意識的認同（專注），這是在你的「知覺專注所在的地方」產生了改變（但是意識仍然是一體）。所以，這是你注意力的「轉換」，也是你認同的「轉換」。

You need nature as your teacher to help you re-connect with Being. But not only do you need nature, it also needs you.

You are not separate from nature. We are all part of the One Life that manifests itself in countless forms throughout the universe, forms that are all completely interconnected. When you recognize the sacredness, the beauty, the incredible stillness and dignity in which a flower or a tree exists, you add something to the flower or the tree. Through your recognition, your awareness, nature too comes to know itself. It comes to know its own beauty and sacredness through you!

A great silent space holds all of nature in its embrace. It also holds you.

∫

　　你要以自然為師，以便與本體重新連結。但並非你單方面
需要自然，自然也需要你。

　　你與自然並不是分離的，我們全都是宇宙共同生命的一部
分，這共同生命體將自己顯化為無以計數的形狀物事，彼此緊
密相連。當你認出一朵花、一棵樹是透過如此神聖、美麗，且
不可思議的寂照與莊嚴而存在時，你便為這樹、這花增添了些
什麼。透過你的認知與你的覺性，自然也慢慢認識它自己。因
為你，它開始明白了自己的美麗與神聖。

∫

　　一個宏闊的靜寂空間，把自然萬物納於它的懷裡，其中當
然也包括了你。

∫

Only when you are still inside do you have access to the realm of stillness that rocks, plants, and animals inhabit. Only when your noisy mind subsides can you connect with nature at a deep level and go beyond the sense of separation created by excessive thinking.

Thinking is a stage in the evolution of life. Nature exists in innocent stillness that is prior to the arising of thought. The tree, the flower, the bird, the rock are unaware of their own beauty and sacredness. When human beings become still, they go beyond thought. There is an added dimension of knowing, of awareness, in the stillness that is beyond thought.

Nature can bring you to stillness. That is its gift to you. When you perceive and join with nature in the field of stillness, that field becomes permeated with your awareness. That is your gift to nature.

Through you nature becomes aware of itself. Nature has been waiting for you, as it were, for millions of years.

　　唯有內在寂靜下來，你才可能真正進入岩石、植物、動物所安住的寂照之中；唯有喧鬧的心智沉靜了，你才可能擺脫過度思考所帶來的分離感，並在內心深處與自然真正連結。

　　思考是生命演化的一個階段，自然存在於思維生起前的單純寂照之中。那樹、花、鳥、岩石，並未覺察到自己的美麗與神聖。當人寂靜下來，人就超越了思維，就在這超越思維的寂照之中，出現了一個新的境界，一個了悟的、覺知的境界。

　　自然可以引你來到寂照之境，那是它送給你的禮物。當你於此寂照中，深刻感受並與自然相結合之後，那裡將充滿了你的覺性，那是你送給自然的禮物。

　　透過你，自然覺察到它自己。千萬年來，自然一直在等待著你。

關係

Relationships

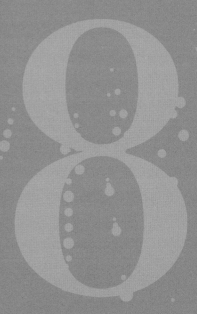

How quick we are to form an opinion of a person, to come to a conclusion about them. It is satisfying to the egoic mind to label another human being, to give them a conceptual identity, to pronounce righteous judgment upon them.

Every human being has been conditioned to think and behave in certain ways — conditioned genetically as well as by their childhood experiences and their cultural environment.

That is not who they are, but that is who they appear to be. When you pronounce judgment upon someone, you confuse those conditioned mind patterns with who they are. To do that is in itself a deeply conditioned and unconscious pattern. You give them a conceptual identity, and that false identity becomes a prison not only for the other person but also for yourself.

To let go of judgment does not mean that you don't see what they do. It means that you recognize their behavior as a form of conditioning, and you see it and accept it as that. You don't construct an identity out of it for that person.

$\int$

　　我們是多麼容易就對別人有了看法，並且對他們做出論斷。小我最樂意去做的事就是往別人身上貼標籤，給別人一個概念化的身分，還宣稱這是公正的評斷。

　　人的思考與行為在某些方面都是被制約的，被遺傳基因、童年經驗以及文化環境所制約。

　　但那並不是人們真正的樣子，只是他們表面看起來如此。所以，當你對別人發出評斷時，你是將別人受制約的心智表現與真正的他混淆了。你這麼做的本身，也是種被嚴重制約、無意識的心智模式。你加諸別人一個概念化的身分，這個虛假的身分變成了牢籠，不僅囚禁了他們，也囚禁了你自己。

　　不去評斷別人，並不是不再看他人的所作所為，而是你明白他們的行為都只是受制約的表現，你看見了，也如實地接受，並且不再從這些行為表現去為對方建構一個虛假的身分。

∫

That liberates you as well as the other person from identification with conditioning, with form, with mind. The ego then no longer runs your relationships.

As long as the ego runs your life, most of your thoughts, emotions, and actions arise from desire and fear. In relationships you then either want or fear something from the other person.

What you want from them may be pleasure or material gain, recognition, praise or attention, or a strengthening of your sense of self through comparison and through establishing that you are, have, or know more than they. What you fear is that the opposite may be the case, and they may diminish your sense of self in some way.

When you make the present moment the focal point of your attention — instead of using it as a means to an end — you go beyond the ego and beyond the unconscious compulsion to use people as a means to an end, the end being self-enhancement at the cost of others. When you give your fullest attention to whoever you are interacting with, you take past and future out of the relationship, except for practical matters. When you are fully present with everyone you meet, you relinquish the conceptual identity you made for them — your interpretation of who they are and what they did in the past — and are able to interact without the egoic movements of desire and fear. Attention, which is alert stillness, is the key.

　　這會讓你和對方都得到解放，從此不再認同於外相、心智與受制約的反應，於是你的小我也就無法再主導你的人際關係了。

　　只要是小我在主導你的生命，你絕大部分的想法、情緒與行動都會出自欲望與恐懼；於是在人際關係裡，你要不就是想從別人身上得到些什麼，要不就是害怕著別人的什麼。

　　你想從他人身上得到的東西，也許是愉悅，也許是某項實質利益，或者是別人的認可、讚美與關注，也可以是自我感的鞏固──透過較量及建立身分地位，透過自己擁有的或懂得的比別人多來鞏固。而你所恐懼的東西，則恰好和上述相反，它們可能會在某方面貶抑了你的自我感。

　　當你不再把當下視為達成目的的工具，而把它變為你注意力的焦點，你便超越了小我，也超越了不由自主想利用他人達到某些目的的衝動，超越了以他人為代價來強壯自我。當你全然專注於任何與你互動的人，你們之間，除了處理實際的問題之外，過去和未來都不存在了。當你全然「臨在」於每個遇到的人，你將放棄對他們所作的概念化身分識別，那些你認為他們是誰，過去做了什麼事情的概念詮釋。你們之間的互動，也將不再帶著小我的欲望與恐懼。專注，是充滿醒覺的寂照，它是一切的關鍵。

How wonderful to go beyond wanting and fearing in your relationships. Love does not want or fear anything.

∫

If her past were your past, her pain your pain, her level of consciousness your level of consciousness, you would think and act exactly as she does. With this realization comes forgiveness, compassion, peace.

The ego doesn't like to hear this, because if it cannot be reactive and righteous anymore, it will lose strength.

∫

When you receive whoever comes into the space of Now as a noble guest, when you allow each person to be as they are, they begin to change.

∫

超越欲望與恐懼的人際關係是多麼美好啊！愛，沒有需求，也無懼於任何事物。

如果她的過去就是你的過去，她的痛苦就是你的痛苦，她的意識層次就是你的意識層次，你的所思、所為就會完全和她一樣。有了這樣的了解後，寬恕、慈悲與平靜將油然而生。

小我可不想聽到這些話，因為如果它不再有正當性，無法為反應而反應，小我將會失去力量。

如果她的過去就是你的過去，她的痛苦就是你的痛苦，她的意識層次就是你的意識層次，你的所思、所為就會完全和她一樣。

當你把任何進到「當下」空間的人視為貴客，並且讓他們做他自己，這些人就開始改變了。

To know another human being in their essence, you don't really need to know anything *about* them — their past, their history, their story. We confuse knowing *about* with a deeper knowing that is non-conceptual. Knowing *about* and knowing are totally different modalities. One is concerned with form, the other with the formless. One operates through thought, the other through stillness.

Knowing *about* is helpful for practical purposes. On that level, we cannot do without it. When it is the predominant modality in relationships, however, it becomes very limiting, even destructive. Thoughts and concepts create an artificial barrier, a separation between human beings. Your interactions are then not rooted in Being, but become mind-based. Without the conceptual barriers, love is naturally present in all human interactions.

Most human interactions are confined to the exchange of words — the realm of thought. It is essential to bring some stillness, particularly into your close relationships.

　　若想從本質上去認識一個人，你不需要知道關於他的任何事，例如：他的過去、歷史或故事。我們把對某人的事有「相關性的了解」與非概念化的真正認識弄混了，它們是兩種不同的型態，前者著重在有相，後者著重在無相，前者以思考運作，後者則透過寂照運作。

　　從實際面來說，對某人有「相關性了解」是很有助益的，且不能沒有它。但如果這種相關性了解變成人際關係中的主要型態，它就變得有局限性，甚至具破壞性了。思考與概念在人與人之間製造了一個人為的障礙，於是人際的互動就不是根植於本體，而是以心智為基礎，只有去除掉這個概念柵欄，愛就會自然「臨在」於所有人類的互動中。

　　大部分的人類互動都被限制在言語的交流下，也就是限制在思維的範疇裡。因此，把寂照帶進你的人際關係，特別是親密關係中是非常重要的。

No relationship can thrive without the sense of spaciousness that comes with stillness. Meditate or spend silent time in nature together. When going for a walk or sitting in the car or at home, become comfortable with being in stillness together. Stillness cannot and need not be created. Just be receptive to the stillness that is already there, but is usually obscured by mental noise.

If spacious stillness is missing, the relationship will be dominated by the mind and can easily be taken over by problems and conflict. If stillness is there, it can contain anything.

∫

True listening is another way of bringing stillness into the relationship. When you truly listen to someone, the dimension of stillness arises and becomes an essential part of the relationship. But true listening is a rare skill. Usually, the greater part of a person's attention is taken up by their thinking. At best, they may be evaluating your words or preparing the next thing to say. Or they may not be listening at all, lost in their own thoughts.

任何的關係，如果缺乏了伴隨寂照而來的無垠寬廣的感受，便無法成長茁壯。與親友一起在自然中冥想或共度安靜時光，不論是外出散步，或是安坐於車上或家裡，你們都將因為共同「臨在」於寂照之中，而感到輕鬆自在。寂照，是無法也不需去創造的，它本已存在，你只要好好感受並接納它。不過，它總是被我們的心智雜音所干擾。

如果那無垠的寂照消失了，人際關係就會淪為由心智所掌控，而且輕易地被問題與衝突所接管。如果寂照存在，它將包容所有的一切。

真正的傾聽，是另一個將寂照帶入人際關係的方法。當你真正在傾聽別人說話時，寂照的層面將會自然生起，變成了人際關係中很重要的部分。但是，真正的傾聽是種少見的技能，人們大部分的注意力，通常都被自己的想法所佔滿了。好一點的，也只是在衡量你說的話，準備下一句要說什麼，當然，他們更可能完全沒在聽，迷失在自己的念頭裡。

True listening goes far beyond auditory perception. It is the arising of alert attention, a space of presence in which the words are being received. The words now become secondary. They may be meaningful or they may not make sense. Far more important than *what* you are listening to is the act of listening itself, the space of conscious presence that arises as you listen. That space is a unifying field of awareness in which you meet the other person without the separative barriers created by conceptual thinking. And now the other person is no longer "other." In that space, you are joined together as one awareness, one consciousness.

Do you experience frequent and repetitive drama in your close relationships? Do relatively insignificant disagreements often trigger violent arguments and emotional pain?

At the root of such experiences lie the basic egoic patterns: the need to be right and, of course, for someone else to be wrong; that is to say, identification with mental positions. There is also the ego's need to be periodically in conflict with something or someone in order to strengthen its sense of separation between "me" and the "other" without which it cannot survive.

　　真正的傾聽，遠遠超越了聽覺的感知。真正傾聽是警醒的專注力的生起，並形成一個「臨在」空間接收話語，這時語詞變得次要，它們也許有意義，也許完全沒道理，重要的是傾聽本身這個行為，與當你傾聽時，所生起的那個「臨在」空間，而不是你聽到對方說些什麼。這空間是意識成為一體的地方，在這空間裡，概念性思維所形成的柵欄不再阻隔人與人之間的相遇，他人不再是「別人」了，你們在這裡結合為一體的覺性、一體的意識。

$$\int$$

　　在親密關係當中，是否經常上演重複的戲碼？是否經常因為芝麻綠豆的小事，引發激烈的爭論與情緒上的痛苦？

　　這一切皆根源於基本的小我模式：我是「對」的。當然，還必須有個犯錯的他人。換句話說，就是認同於心智的立場。此外，還有個小我的基本需求是，要週期性的與某人或某事有所衝突，藉以強調「人」、「我」之間是有區別的。少了這些衝突，小我就無法存在。

In addition, there is the accumulated emotional pain from the past that you and each human being carries within, both from your personal past as well as the collective pain of humanity that goes back a long, long time. This "pain-body" is an energy field within you that sporadically takes you over because it needs to experience more emotional pain for it to feed on and replenish itself. It will try to control your thinking and make it deeply negative. It loves your negative thoughts, since it resonates with their frequency and so can feed on them. It will also provoke negative emotional reactions in people close to you, especially your partner, in order to feed on the ensuing drama and emotional pain.

How can you free yourself from this deep-seated unconscious identification with pain that creates so much misery in your life?

Become aware of it. Realize that it is not who you are, and recognize it for what it is: past pain. Witness it as it happens in your partner or in yourself. When your unconscious identification with it is broken, when you are able to observe it within yourself, you don't feed it anymore, and it will gradually lose its energy charge.

　　此外，每個人心中都帶著從過去到現在所累積下來的情緒傷痛，它們來自你個人的過去，也來自人類久遠以來的集體痛苦。此一「痛苦之身」是你內在的一個能量場，它不時地來佔有你，因為它靠感受更多的痛苦來餵養與填滿自己。「痛苦之身」企圖控制你的思考，讓你的想法變得極端負面，它愛你的負面想法，因為頻率相同，它能賴以為食。它還會在你所親近的人們身上煽起負面的情緒反應，尤其是你的伴侶，藉此餵養接下來的戲碼與情緒痛苦。

　　你要如何擺脫這在你生命中製造了無數不幸，根深柢固的、對痛苦的無意識認同感？

　　覺察那痛苦，明白那痛苦並非真正的你，並且認清它的真面目：過去的痛苦。當痛苦發生於你的伴侶或自己身上時，看著它。當你不再無意識地認同於它，當你能夠於內在觀察它，你就不再餵養它了，而它也將逐漸失去了能量的補充。

Human interaction can be hell. Or it can be a great spiritual practice.

∫

When you look upon another human being and feel great love toward them, or when you contemplate beauty in nature and something within you responds deeply to it, close your eyes for a moment and feel the essence of that love or that beauty within you, inseparable from who you are, your true nature. The outer form is a temporary reflection of what you are within, in your essence. That is why love and beauty can never leave you, although all outer forms will.

∫

What is your relationship with the world of objects, the countless things that surround you and that you handle every day? The chair you sit on, the pen, the car, the cup? Are they to you merely a means to an end, or do you occasionally acknowledge their existence, their being, no matter how briefly, by noticing them and giving them your attention?

人類彼此的互動，可以是煉獄，也可以成為偉大的靈性修行。

∫

當你看著一個人，並感到有極大愛湧向他們，或當你凝視自然的美好，內在與之深深呼應時，請將雙眼闔上片刻，去感受你內在那股愛和美的本質，去感受它們與真正的你或你的本性是如此地密不可分。外在形相是你內在本質的暫時映現，因此，外在形相早晚會消失，而愛與美卻永遠不會離你而去。

∫

你與這個物質世界，以及那些每天包圍著你、必須處理的眾多事物，關係如何呢？你坐的那張椅子、那支筆、那輛車、那只杯子……它們對你來說，只是工具嗎？偶爾，無論多麼短暫，你會因為瞥見它們，對它們起了關注，進而認識到它們的存在、它們的本體嗎？

When you get attached to objects, when you are using them to enhance your worth in your own eyes and in the eyes of others, concern about things can easily take over your whole life. When there is self-identification with things, you don't appreciate them for what they are because you are looking for yourself in them.

When you appreciate an object for what it is, when you acknowledge its being without mental projection, you cannot *not* feel grateful for its existence. You may also sense that it is not really inanimate, that it only appears so to the senses. Physicists will confirm that on a molecular level it is indeed a pulsating energy field.

Through selfless appreciation of the realm of things, the world around you will come alive in ways that you cannot even begin to comprehend with the mind.

∫

Whenever you meet anyone, no matter how briefly, do you acknowledge their being by giving them your full attention? Or are you reducing them to a means to an end, a mere function or role?

當你對於事物產生了執著，當你利用它們提升你在自己與他人眼中的價值，這種對於外在事物的在意，便能輕易地佔據你全部的生命。當你的自我認同來自於外在事物，你將不再欣賞這些東西的本然面貌，因為你只是在它們身上尋找你自己罷了！

當你欣賞一件物品的本然樣貌，當你不帶任何心智投射的眼光認識它的本體，你無可避免地會感謝它的存在。你也許感覺到它並非真的是無生命，只是對我們的感官來說是如此。物理學家將證實，從分子層次來看，它實際上是一個正在搏動的能量場。

若從無我的角度欣賞事物的世界，你周遭的一切，將會以你連想去思維都無從思維起的方式，而活了起來。

不論遇到任何人，不管相處時間是多麼短暫，你是否都能以完整的關注去認識他們的本體？或者，你只是把他們當成為達到某種目的的工具、某種功能或角色？

What is the quality of your relationship with the cashier at the supermarket, the parking attendant, the repairman, the "customer"?

A moment of attention is enough. As you look at them or listen to them, there is an alert stillness — perhaps only two or three seconds, perhaps longer. That is enough for something more real to emerge than the roles we usually play and identify with. All roles are part of the conditioned consciousness that is the human mind. That which emerges through the act of attention is the un- conditioned — who you are in your essence, underneath your name and form. You are no longer acting out a script; you become real. When that dimension emerges from within you, it also draws it forth from within the other person.

Ultimately, of course, there is no other, and you are always meeting yourself.

　　你與超市收銀員、停車場管理員、修理工人或「顧客」的
互動關係品質如何？

　　只要片刻的專注便已足夠，就在你凝視或傾聽他們的時
候，一種警醒的靜觀寂照生起，也許只有兩、三秒，也許再久
一點，那便足讓某些更為真實的東西顯現出來，它比我們平常
所扮演與認同的角色真實。所有的角色，都是被制約的意識，
也就是人類心智的一部分；那因為專注而顯現的一切則是不
受制約的——是隱藏在你的名字與外在形相之下，你的真正本
質。你不再依照人生劇本演出；你變得真實。當這個層面自你
內在浮現出來時，它同時也將其他人的相同內在召喚出來。

　　最後，很自然地，不再有別人了，你總是遇見你自己。

死亡與永恆

Death & the Eternal

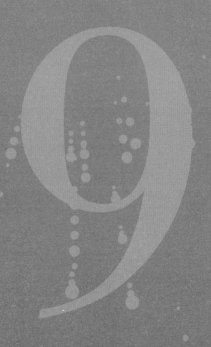

When you walk through a forest that has not been tamed and interfered with by man, you will see not only abundant life all around you, but you will also encounter fallen trees and decaying trunks, rotting leaves and decomposing matter at every step. Wherever you look, you will find death as well as life.

Upon closer scrutiny, however, you will discover that the decomposing tree trunk and rotting leaves not only give birth to new life, but are full of life themselves. Microorganisms are at work. Molecules are rearranging themselves. So death isn't to be found any where. There is only the metamorphosis of life forms. What can you learn from this?

Death is not the opposite of life. Life has no opposite. The opposite of death is birth. Life is eternal.

$$\int$$

Sages and poets throughout the ages have recognized the dreamlike quality of human existence — seemingly so solid and real and yet so fleeting that it could dissolve at any moment.

　　穿越一座尚未為人類所開發與干擾的森林，你看見的將不只是周遭豐沛的生命，同時也會有倒木和枯幹，舉步之間，處處皆是腐葉與正在分解的物質。無論你往哪邊看去，都會看到生命，同時也發現死亡。

　　然而，若是上前仔細檢查，你將發現那些分解中的樹幹及腐葉，不僅帶來新的生命，它們本身也充滿了生氣。微生物正努力工作，分子們也正自我重組中。所以，哪裡都找不到死亡，只有生命型態的不同變態。你，從這一切學到了什麼？

　　生命的相對並非死亡，生命是沒有對立面的。死亡的相對是誕生，生命是永恆的。

$$\int$$

　　自古以來的聖賢哲人與詩人墨客，都曾道破人的存在有著如夢似幻的特質，它看起來如此地堅固與真實，卻又如此地短暫，能於轉瞬間煙消雲散。

At the hour of your death, the story of your life may, indeed, appear to you like a dream that is coming to an end. Yet even in a dream there must be an essence that is real. There must be a consciousness in which the dream happens; otherwise, it would not be.

That consciousness — does the body create it or does consciousness create the dream of body, the dream of somebody?

Why have most of those who went through a near-death experience lost their fear of death? Reflect upon this.

∫

Of course you know you are going to die, but that remains a mere mental concept until you meet death "in person" for the first time: through a serious illness or an accident that happens to you or someone close to you, or through the passing away of a loved one, death enters your life as the awareness of your own mortality.

　　瀕於死亡之時，你一生的故事確實有可能感覺像夢一般地即將結束。然而即使在夢中，也必然有真實不虛的本質，必得有意識的存在，夢才能於其中發生；否則，哪裡會有夢呢？

　　究竟是身體創造了這意識？或是意識夢見了身體、意識夢見了有某個人*？

　　為何大部分具有瀕死經驗的人，不再恐懼死亡？為什麼？請仔細想想看！

$$\int$$

　　你當然知道自己正在邁向死亡，但那都僅只是心理上的一個概念，直到有一天你「親身」與死亡相遇，也許是你或你身邊的人得了重病或發生意外，也許是摯愛的人辭世，你才覺知到自己也不免一死，這時死亡便進入了你的生命。

---

*究竟是身體創造了這意識？或是意識夢見了身體、意識夢見了有某個人？

That consciousness — does the body create it or does consciousness create the dream of body, the dream of somebody?

這裡是在討論關於「雞生蛋」或「蛋生雞」的問題，也就是說，是「身體創造意識」或「意識創造身體」？意識創造「有某個人」，這裡其實指的就是「小我」，夢見有個「我」這個人的存在。所以，一個是肉體上的「我」，一個是概念上的「我」。

Most people turn away from it in fear, but if you do not flinch and face the fact that your body is fleeting and could dissolve at any moment, there is some degree of dis-identification, however slight, from your own physical and psychological form, the "me." When you see and accept the impermanent nature of all life forms, a strange sense of peace comes upon you.

Through facing death, your consciousness is freed to some extent from identification with form. This is why in some Buddhist traditions, the monks regularly visit the morgue to sit and meditate among the dead bodies.

There is still a widespread denial of death in Western cultures. Even old people try not to speak or think about it, and dead bodies are hidden away. A culture that denies death inevitably becomes shallow and superficial, concerned only with the external form of things. When death is denied, life loses its depth. The possibility of knowing who we are beyond name and form, the dimension of the transcendent, disappears from our lives because death is the opening into that dimension.

∫

　　大多數人在面對死亡時，會因恐懼而別過頭去，但如果你不退縮，勇敢地面對肉體是暫時的，極可能在任何一刻消失，那麼，你多少會對自己生理與心理上那表相的「我」，有某種程度的「認同解構」。當你了解並接受所有生命型態都是無常的，一種奇異的內在平安感便降臨了。

　　藉由面對死亡，你的意識將在某種程度上，擺脫了對於表相的認同。所以，在有些佛教傳統中，僧侶才會定期造訪停屍之處，並在屍體之間打坐與禪修。

　　在西方文化之中，還是普遍存在著對於死亡的否定，即使是老人也避諱去談論或思考死亡，死去的軀體更被遠遠地藏了起來。一個不承認死亡的文化，必然會變得膚淺與迷信，變得只在意事物的表相。否定了死亡，生命將失去它的深度，我們將失去了解那名稱與表相之後的自己究竟是誰的可能性，我們更失去了解那超越一般人類心智經驗的境界的機會，因為死亡就是通往那裡的一扇門。

People tend to be uncomfortable with endings, because every ending is a little death. That's why in many languages, the word for "good-bye" means "see you again."

Whenever an experience comes to an end — a gathering of friends, a vacation, your children leaving home — you die a little death. A "form" that appeared in your consciousness as that experience dissolves. Often this leaves behind a feeling of emptiness that most people try hard not to feel, not to face.

If you can learn to accept and even welcome the endings in your life, you may find that the feeling of emptiness that initially felt uncomfortable turns into a sense of inner spaciousness that is deeply peaceful.

By learning to die daily in this way, you open yourself to Life.

∫

Most people feel that their identity, their sense of self, is something incredibly precious that they don't want to lose. That is why they have such fear of death.

　　人們對於各種「結束」總是感到不自在，因為每個結束都是一次小的死亡。這就是為何在許多不同的語言之中，「再見」這個字的意思是指「下次再見到你」的原因。

　　朋友聚會、假期、孩子要離家了，無論何時，事情每到了尾聲，你也小小地「死」了一次。你的意識之中會生起一個「感受」，而那通常是一種「空虛」的感覺，大多數人都努力不去感覺它，不去面對它。

　　如果你可以學著去接受，甚或迎接生命的結束，你或許將發現那原本讓你不自在的「空虛」感，已轉化成一種深沉平安，內在寬廣無垠的感受。

　　每天學著這樣死去，你對生命就開放了。

　　大多數人認為自己的身分、自我感，是極其珍貴且不能失去的東西，因此，他們對死亡是如此地恐懼。

It seems unimaginable and frightening that "I" could cease to exist. But you confuse that precious "I" with your name and form and a story associated with it. That "I" is no more than a temporary formation in the field of consciousness.

As long as that form identity is all you know, you are not aware that this preciousness is your own essence, your innermost sense of *I Am* , which is consciousness itself. It is the eternal in you — and that's the only thing you *cannot* lose.

∫

Whenever any kind of deep loss occurs in your life — such as loss of possessions, your home, a close relationship; or loss of your reputation, job, or physical abilities — something inside you dies. You feel diminished in your sense of who you are. There may also be a certain disorientation. "Without this...who am I?"

When a form that you had unconsciously identified with as part of yourself leaves you or dissolves, that can be extremely painful. It leaves a hole, so to speak, in the fabric of your existence.

　　「我」的存在終止了，這似乎無法想像，又讓人害怕。其實，你把那珍貴的「我」與我的名字、我的形相身體和我的故事搞混了。那個「我」充其量不過就是意識場上一個暫時的構成罷了！

　　如果你所知道的只是對這些對外在形相的認同，那你就尚未覺察到，最珍貴的其實是你的本體，是你內心深處「我本是」的存在感，也就是意識本身。它是你內在的永恆，也是你唯一不會失去的東西。

　　生命中如果發生了嚴重的損失，例如失去財產、你的家、一段親密關係；或者失去你的名聲、工作或身體功能等，你內在某些東西也會死去。你的自我感會縮小，甚至還會有些迷惘：「沒有了這些……，我是誰？」

　　那個在你無意識的狀況下被認定為自己的一部分的有形的我，如果棄你而去，或化為烏有，會造成極大的痛苦，好像是在你的存在結構上，留下了一個空洞。

When this happens, don't deny or ignore the pain or the sadness that you feel. Accept that it is there. Beware of your mind's tendency to construct a story around that loss in which you are assigned the role of victim. Fear, anger, resentment, or self- pity are the emotions that go with that role. Then become aware of what lies behind those emotions as well as behind the mind-made story: that hole, that empty space. Can you face and accept that strange sense of emptiness? If you do, you may find that it is no longer a fearful place. You may be surprised to find peace emanating from it.

Whenever death occurs, whenever a life form dissolves, God, the formless and un-manifested, shines through the opening left by the dissolving form. That is why the most sacred thing in life is death. That is why the peace of God can come to you through the contemplation and acceptance of death.

∫

How short-lived every human experience is, how fleeting our lives. Is there anything that is not subject to birth and death, anything that is eternal?

　　當它發生了，請不要否定或忽略你所感受到的痛苦或悲傷，接納這一切，謹防心智據此損失建構出一個故事，一個你在其中扮演受害者角色的故事，恐懼、生氣、怨恨或自卑，都將伴隨此角色而來。請覺察在這些情緒與由心智所打造的故事背後隱藏了什麼：那個空洞，那個什麼都沒有的空間。你能夠面對並接納那「空」所帶來的奇異感受嗎？如果你真的可以，你就會有可能發現那「空」不再是個令人害怕的地方，甚至能驚訝地發現從那之中所散發出的平靜安詳。

　　無論死亡何時發生，無論生命形體何時消失，神——那無形無相、未顯化的狀態，將透過形體消散後留下的開放空間發出光芒。那就是為何生命中最神聖的事情就是死亡，那也是為何神的平安，可以透過沉思和接納死亡，來到你面前。

$$\int$$

　　人的經歷是如此短暫，生命轉瞬即逝，有什麼是不受限於生死的？有什麼是永恆的？

Consider this: if there were only one color, let us say blue, and the entire world and everything in it were blue, then there would be no blue. There needs to be something that is not blue so that blue can be recognized; otherwise, it would not "stand out," would not exist.

In the same way, does it not require something that is not fleeting and impermanent for the fleetingness of all things to be recognized? In other words: if everything, including yourself, were impermanent, would you even know it? Does the fact that you are aware of and can witness the short-lived nature of all forms, including your own, not mean that there is something in you that is not subject to decay?

When you are twenty, you are aware of your body as strong and vigorous; sixty years later, you are aware of your body as weakened and old. Your thinking too may have changed from when you were twenty, but the awareness that knows that your body is young or old or that your thinking has changed has undergone no change. That awareness is the eternal in you — consciousness itself. It is the formless One Life. Can you lose It? No, because you are It.

　　想想看，如果世上只有一種顏色，假設是藍色，整個世界與其中所有一切都是藍色，那藍色就不再是藍色了。必須要有某樣不是藍色的東西，藍色才能被襯托出來；否則，它將無法「顯現」，無法存在。

　　同樣地，不也必須有某些並非短暫、不持久的東西，才能讓人們認清萬事萬物皆是無常的？換句話說，如果所有的一切，包括你自己，都是轉瞬即逝的，你還能知道這些嗎？你從萬物無常的本質，從你自己身上所覺知到的、所見證到的真理，不正意味著你內在存在著某些東西，是永不衰去的嗎？

　　二十歲時，你覺得自己身強體壯、精力充沛；六十年後，你覺得自己既衰老且虛弱。你的想法可能也和身體一樣，自二十歲以來改變了許多，但是那覺知到身體是年輕或衰老，覺知到想法已改變的覺性本身，卻從未改變，那覺性是你內在的永恆，是意識本身。它是無形無相的宇宙共同生命，你會失去它嗎？不會，因為你就是它。

Some people become deeply peaceful and almost luminous just before they die, as if something is shining through the dissolving form.

Sometimes it happens that very ill or old people become almost transparent, so to speak, in the last few weeks, months, or even years of their lives. As they look at you, you may see a light shining through their eyes. There is no psychological suffering left. They have surrendered and so the person, the mind-made egoic "me," has already dissolved. They have "died before they died" and found the deep inner peace that is the realization of the deathless within themselves.

∫

To every accident and disaster there is a potentially redemptive dimension that we are usually unaware of.

　　有些人臨終前十分平靜安詳，甚至透著光彩，好似有什麼東西從他那即將消逝的形體裡照射出來。

　　有時，在一些重症患者或老人身上，也可看到他們在生命的最後數周、數月，甚至數年之間，變得清透。當他們凝視著你，你可能會看見他們眼中閃耀著光芒。那裡沒有了精神上的痛苦，他們已然臣服了，而那個心智小我也已然消失不見。他們在「死前先死過」了，並找到了內心深處的平安，了悟了他們自己內在是永恆不朽的。

$$\int$$

　　每件意外與災難，都存在著一個可能的救贖，我們卻經常未能察覺。

The tremendous shock of totally unexpected, imminent death can have the effect of forcing your consciousness completely out of identification with form. In the last few moments before physical death, and as you die, you then experience yourself as consciousness free of form. Suddenly, there is no more fear, just peace and a knowing that "all is well" and that death is only a form dissolving. Death is then recognized as ultimately illusory — as illusory as the form you had identified with as yourself.

Death is not an anomaly or the most dreadful of all events as modern culture would have you believe, but the most natural thing in the world, inseparable from and just as natural as its polarity — birth. Remind yourself of this when you sit with a dying person.

It is a great privilege and a sacred act to be present at a person's death as a witness and companion.

When you sit with a dying person, do not deny any aspect of that experience. Do not deny what is happening and do not deny your feelings. The recognition that there is nothing you can do may make you feel helpless, sad,

突如其來的死亡所帶來的震撼，將迫使你的意識脫離對形相的認同。肉體死亡前的最後時刻，以及死亡的那一刻，你將體驗到自己不再是那軀殼，而是意識本身。剎那間，再也沒有恐懼，只有平靜以及知道「一切安好」，知道了死亡只是形體的消失。死亡於是被認出來它終究是虛幻不實的，就像你曾認同過的形體一樣虛幻不實。

死亡並不像現代文明要你相信的那樣，是違反常態，或是人生中最可怕的事。其實，它是世上最自然不過的一件事，與它所對應的「生」同樣自然，而且密不可分。當你坐在瀕死之人身旁，請記得這點。

見證並陪伴他人步向死亡，是神聖的行為，更是莫大的恩典。

當你坐在瀕死之人身旁，不要對這經歷有任何的否定，不要否定正在發生的事情，也不要否定你的感覺。發現自己幫不上忙，或許讓你感到無助、難過或生氣，但你要接納這樣的感受，然後更進一步地，接納自己的無能為力，徹底全然地接納。事情不受你主導，深深地臣服於眼前的一切與你的感覺，

or angry. Accept what you feel. Then go one step further: accept that there is nothing you can do, and accept it completely. You are not in control. Deeply surrender to every aspect of that experience, your feelings as well as any pain or discomfort the dying person may be experiencing. Your surrendered state of consciousness and the stillness that comes with it will greatly assist the dying person and ease their transition. If words are called for, they will come out of the stillness within you. But they will be secondary.

With the stillness comes the benediction: peace.

以及臣服於那瀕死之人可能經歷的任何痛苦或不適。寂照伴隨
著你已臣服的意識狀態，將會對臨終者助益良多，而使得這段
死亡的轉化過程更容易一些。若有必要說話，那也必發自你內
心深處的寂照，但那不是最重要的。

　　隨著寂照而來的是祝禱的恩賜──內在深邃的平安。

痛苦與
痛苦的止息
Suffering & the End of Suffering

10

The interconnectedness of all things: Buddhists have always known it, and physicists now confirm it. Nothing that happens is an isolated event; it only appears to be. The more we judge and label it, the more we isolate it. The wholeness of life becomes fragmented through our thinking. Yet the totality of life has brought this event about. It is part of the web of interconnectedness that is the cosmos.

This means: whatever *is* could not be otherwise.

In most cases, we cannot begin to understand what role a seemingly senseless event may have within the totality of the cosmos, but recognizing its inevitability within the vastness of the whole can be the beginning of an inner acceptance of what *is* and thus a realignment with the wholeness of life.

∫

True freedom and the end of suffering is living in such a way as if you had completely chosen whatever you feel or experience at this moment.

This inner alignment with Now is the end of suffering.

∫

　　佛教徒早已知曉萬事萬物是相互依存的，科學家也已證實了這點。世上沒有任何一件事的發生是獨立的，它們只是表面上看起來好像是獨立存在而已。我們愈是用思維去論斷分別它，為它貼上標籤，便愈孤立了那事件。生命的整體性因這許許多多的思維而變得片段破碎，其實，是生命整體的因緣和合讓那事件發生，它是宇宙相互依存網絡的一部分。

　　這也意味著：萬物本來是什麼就是什麼，不可能是別的。

　　一般來說，我們無法去了解那些看似毫無意義的事件，可能在宇宙整體中扮演怎樣的角色，除非你認出它在廣袤的整體中的必然存在性，你才有可能打心底開始去接納這件事的本來面貌，於是，你與生命整體重新結盟。

　　把當下的感受或經驗完全都當成好像是自己選擇的，這樣地過活，就是真正的自由與痛苦的止息。

　　在心中與當下結盟，就是痛苦的止息。

Is suffering really necessary? Yes and no.

If you had not suffered as you have, there would be no depth to you as a human being, no humility, no compassion. You would not be reading this now. Suffering cracks open the shell of ego, and then comes a point when it has served its purpose. Suffering is necessary until you realize it is unnecessary.

∫

Unhappiness needs a mind-made "me" with a story, the conceptual identity. It needs time — past and future. When you remove time from your unhappiness, what is it that remains? The "suchness" of this moment remains.

It may be a feeling of heaviness, agitation, tightness, anger, or even nausea. That is not unhappiness, and it is not a personal problem. There is nothing personal in human pain. It is simply an intense pressure or intense energy that you feel somewhere in the body. By giving it attention, the feeling doesn't turn into thinking and thus reactivate the unhappy "me."

See what happens when you just allow a feeling to be.

受苦真的是必要的嗎？是，也不是。

如果你未曾經歷你所經歷的痛苦，那麼你將不具備身為一個人的深度，不會懂得謙虛，不懂得慈悲，你也不會現在聽著這些話了。痛苦將小我的硬殼敲破，這時它的目的也就達到了。痛苦是必要的，直到你明白了它並非必要為止。

∫

「不快樂」需要一個由心智所打造的「我」的故事，一個概念上的身分；「不快樂」還需要時間——過去與未來。當你將時間從「不快樂」當中抽離了，還剩下什麼？那就是此刻的「本然狀況」。

它也許是一種沉重、不安、壓迫、生氣或極端憎惡的感覺，卻不是不快樂，也不是個人的問題。人類的痛苦皆非個人的，那只是一種於你體內某處感受到的強烈壓力或能量，你只要注意它，不讓那感覺轉化為念頭想法，不快樂的「我」就無法恢復動力。

留心觀察，如果你讓感覺就是感覺，會發生什麼事？

∫

Much suffering, much unhappiness arises when you take each thought that comes into your head for the truth. Situations don't make you unhappy. They may cause you physical pain, but they don't make you unhappy. Your thoughts make you unhappy. Your interpretations, the stories you tell yourself make you unhappy.

"The thoughts I am thinking right now are making me unhappy." This realization breaks your unconscious identification with those thoughts.

∫

What a miserable day.

He didn't have the decency to return my call.

She let me down.

Little stories we tell ourselves and others, often in the form of complaints. They are unconsciously designed to enhance our always deficient sense of self through being "right" and making something or someone "wrong". Being

∫

　　那麼多的痛苦與不快樂，都是因為你將每個進到大腦裡的想法都當真了。事情的狀況不會讓你不快樂，它們頂多引起一些生理上的不舒服，但不會讓你不快樂，是你的想法造成你的不快樂，是那些你對狀況的看法，你說給自己聽的故事，讓你不快樂。

　　「是我此刻的想法，讓我不快樂。」有了這點醒悟，你就擺脫了自己不自覺中對那些想法的認同。

∫

　　真是糟透了的一天！

　　他真沒禮貌，竟然不回我電話。

　　她太讓我失望了。

　　通常，我們都是用抱怨的方式，述說這些小故事給自己或別人聽。我們不自覺地將這些故事設計成自己是「對」的，別人或事情是「錯」的，藉此加強我們那總覺得匱乏的自我感。

"right" places us in a position of imagined superiority and so strengthens our false sense of self, the ego. This also creates some kind of enemy: yes, the ego needs enemies to define its boundary, and even the weather can serve that function.

Through habitual mental judgment and emotional contraction, you have a personalized reactive relationship to people and events in your life. These are all forms of self-created suffering, but they are not recognized as such because to the ego they are satisfying. The ego enhances itself through reactivity and conflict.

How simple life would be without those stories.

It is raining.

He did not call.

I was there. She was not.

∫

When you are suffering, when you are unhappy, stay totally with what is Now. Unhappiness or problems cannot survive in the Now.

∫

「我是對的」，讓我們置身於一個想像的優越感之中，因而鞏固了虛假的自我——小我；這同時也塑造了某些做「錯」了的敵人，沒錯，小我是需要敵人來劃定自己的界線，就算拿天氣出氣也可以。

因為慣於在心智上做論斷分別，因為情緒緊繃，你生命中出現的人或事，與你形成了一種個人化的慣性反應式關係，這些全是自尋苦惱，但因為它可以滿足了小我，所以人們並不覺得是苦惱。小我透過慣性反應與衝突分歧，鞏固了它自己。

如果沒有這些故事，生命會是多麼簡單啊！

下雨了。

他沒打電話來。

我到了那裡，但她沒來。

當你痛苦時，當你感到不快樂時，請全然臨於當下。所有不快樂或苦惱，都難以在當下活存。

Suffering begins when you mentally name or label a situation in some way as undesirable or bad. You resent a situation and that resentment personalizes it and brings in a reactive "me."

Naming and labeling are habitual, but that habit can be broken. Start practicing "not naming" with small things. If you miss the plane, drop and break a cup, or slip and fall in the mud, can you refrain from naming the experience as bad or painful? Can you immediately accept the "isness" of that moment?

Naming something as bad causes an emotional contraction within you. When you let it be, without naming it, enormous power is suddenly available to you.

The contraction cuts you off from that power, the power of life itself.

∫

They ate the fruit of the tree of the knowledge of good and evil.

Go beyond good and bad by refraining from mentally labeling anything as good or bad. When you go beyond the habitual naming, the power of the universe moves

　　當你內心認定某件事是討厭的或不好的時候，痛苦便產生了。你厭惡某種處境，這厭惡被個人化，並帶來慣性的「我」。

　　我們總是習慣去認定事情的好壞，但這習慣是可以破除的。一開始，你可以利用一些小事，練習「不去貼標籤」。如你錯過班機、滑落或打破杯子，或是在泥濘中滑倒、摔跤，你可以試著克制自己不給這些事貼上「討厭」或「糟糕」的標籤嗎？你可以立即接納那一刻的「本來如是」嗎？

　　認定某件事是不好的，將讓你陷入情緒緊繃的狀態。一旦順其自然，不再為事情貼上好或壞的標籤，你將發現一股極為強大的力量突然湧現。

　　情緒緊繃讓你自絕於那力量之外，那生命本身的力量之外。

　　他們吃下了善惡知識樹上的果實。

　　只要不再於心裡為任何事情貼上好或壞的標籤，便超越了好與壞。一旦超越自己對事情好壞的慣性認定，宇宙的力量將透過你開始運行。由於你可以對自己所經歷的各種情況，保持一種「不起情緒反應」的關係，那些曾經被你認為是「壞」的

through you. When you are in a nonreactive relationship to experiences, what you would have called "bad" before often turns around quickly, if not immediately, through the power of life itself.

Watch what happens when you don't name an experience as "bad" and instead bring an inner acceptance, an inner "yes" to it, and so let it be as it is.

Whatever your life situation is, how would you feel if you completely accepted it as it is — right Now?

There are many subtle and not so subtle forms of suffering that are so "normal," they are usually not recognized as suffering and may even feel satisfying to the ego — irritation, impatience, anger, having an issue with something or someone, resentment, complaining.

You can learn to recognize all those forms of suffering as they happen and know: at this moment, I am creating suffering for myself.

經驗，通常會透過生命本身的力量，如果不是立即地改變，也
會迅速地有所轉變。

　　注意觀察當你不再認為某個經驗是「壞」的，而以一種接
納，打心底接納的態度去面對它並順其自然時，事情將會發生
什麼變化？

$$\int$$

　　不管你的人生處境為何，如果你當下能完整地接納它的真
實狀況，你會有何感受呢？

$$\int$$

　　惱怒、不耐煩、生氣、對某人或某事有意見、憤慨、抱怨
等小痛苦，或者也不那麼小，它們看起來如此「正常」，以致
一般都不被認為是痛苦，甚至對小我來說，還覺得是滿意的。

　　你可以學著在那些痛苦發生時認出它，並且在心裡明白：
此時此刻，我正在為自己製造痛苦。

If you are in the habit of creating suffering for yourself, you are probably creating suffering for others too. These unconscious mind patterns tend to come to an end simply by making them conscious, by becoming aware of them as they happen.

You cannot be conscious and create suffering for yourself.

∫

This is the miracle: behind every condition, person, or situation that appears "bad" or "evil" lies concealed a deeper good. That deeper good reveals itself to you — both within and without— through inner acceptance of what is .

"Resist not evil" is one of the highest truths of humanity.

∫

A dialogue:
Accept what is.
I truly cannot. I'm agitated and angry about this.
Then accept what is.

　　假如你習於為自己製造痛苦，你很可能也會為他人製造痛苦。若想中止這些無意識的心智模式，很簡單，只要讓它們變得是有覺知的，在它們發生時覺察到它們就行了。

　　你不可能在覺察到痛苦時，同時為自己製造痛苦。

∫

　　每個看似「壞」的或「惡」的人、事、際遇的背後，都隱藏了一個更深沉的「善」。那深沉的「善」，在你打心底接納事情本來的狀況時，便會由內到外地向你揭示它自己。這真是奇蹟啊！

　　「不要抗拒不幸」是人類至高真理之一。

∫

　　一段對話：

　　A：接納事情的本來狀況。

　　B：我真的沒辦法。我對這事既激動又生氣。

　　A：那就接納你現在的狀況。

Accept that I'm agitated and angry? Accept that I cannot accept?

Yes. Bring acceptance into your non-acceptance. Bring surrender into your non-surrender. Then see what happens.

Chronic physical pain is one of the harshest teachers you can have. "Resistance is futile" is its teaching.

Nothing could be more normal than an unwillingness to suffer. Yet if you can let go of that unwillingness, and instead allow the pain to be there, you may notice a subtle inner separation from the pain, a space between you and the pain, as it were. This means to suffer consciously, willingly. When you suffer consciously, physical pain can quickly burn up the ego in you, since ego consists largely of resistance. The same is true of extreme physical disability.

You "offer up your suffering to God" is another way of saying this.

B：接受我既激動又生氣？接受那難以接受的事？

A：是的。將接納帶入你的不接納之中；將臣服帶入你的不臣服之中。看看會發生什麼？

慢性的身體疼痛是最嚴厲的人生導師，「抗拒無用」是它所要教導的。

沒有什麼比「不情願受苦」更正常的了。然而，如果你可以放下那個「不情願」，容許痛苦存在，你可能會在痛苦之間，留意到有個細微的內在分界，有個介於你與痛苦之間的空隙一直都在那裡。這意味著你是有意識的，是心甘情願去受苦的。那麼，身體的疼痛將很快地耗盡你的內在小我，因為小我主要是由抗拒所形構的。這對重度的身體殘障而言，也是真的。

「將你的痛苦獻給神」，是從痛苦中解脫的另一種說法。

You don't need to be a Christian to understand the deep universal truth that is contained in symbolic form in the image of the cross.

The cross is a torture instrument. It stands for the most extreme suffering, limitation, and helplessness a human being can encounter. Then suddenly that human being surrenders, suffers willingly, consciously, expressed through the words, "Not my will but Thy will be done." At that moment, the cross, the torture instrument, shows its hidden face: it is also a sacred symbol, a symbol for the divine.

That which seemed to deny the existence of any transcendental dimension to life, through surrender becomes an opening into that dimension.

　　即使不是基督徒，也可以理解十字架這個象徵符號之中所包含的宇宙真理。

　　十字架是古代的一種刑具，它代表了一個人所能遭遇到的最大痛苦，一種全然的無力與無助，突然之間，那個受苦的人臣服了，他心甘情願地、有意識地接受了那個苦，他說出：「不要從我的意思，只要從祢的意思。」*就在這一刻這刑具的十字架，揭開了它隱藏的面目，告諸世人：十字架也是神聖的象徵，它是神性的象徵。

　　那原本似乎否定生命中有任何超越層面存在的十字架，透過臣服，變成了通往超越的入口。

＊不要從我的意思，只要從祢的意思 Not my will but Thy will be done.
在《聖經》的〈馬太福音〉、〈馬可福音〉與〈路加福音〉中均提到耶穌在最後的晚餐之後，前往客西馬尼園禱告，這句話出自耶穌在面對即將發生的事時，對神所做的禱詞。

BC1006T

當下的覺醒：你到底是誰？啟動意識的更高層次
Stillness Speaks

作者	艾克哈特・托勒（Eckhart Tolle）
譯者	劉永毅
責任編輯	田哲榮
美術構成	吉松薛爾

發行人	蘇拾平
總編輯	于芝峰
副總編輯	田哲榮
業務發行	王綬晨、邱紹溢、劉文雅
行銷企劃	陳詩婷
出版	橡實文化 ACORN Publishing
	地址：231030新北市新店區北新路三段207-3號5樓
	電話：（02）8913-1005 傳真：（02）8913-1056
	網址：www.acornbooks.com.tw
	E-mail信箱：acorn@andbooks.com.tw

發行	大雁出版基地
	地址：231030新北市新店區北新路三段207-3號5樓
	電話：（02）8913-1005 傳真：（02）8913-1056
	讀者服務信箱：andbooks@andbooks.com.tw
	劃撥帳號：19983379 戶名：大雁文化事業股份有限公司

印刷	中原造像股份有限公司
三版一刷	2023年 4 月
三版二刷	2024年 1 月
定價	320元
ISBN	978-626-7085-83-7

國家圖書館出版品預行編目（CIP）資料

當下的覺醒：你到底是誰？啟動意識的更高層次/艾克哈
特・托勒（Eckhart Tolle）著；劉永毅譯. -- 三版. -- 臺北
市：橡實文化出版：大雁出版基地發行, 2023.04
208面；15×21公分
譯自：Stillness speaks

ISBN 978-626-7085-83-7(平裝)
1.CST：靈修

192.1   112001799

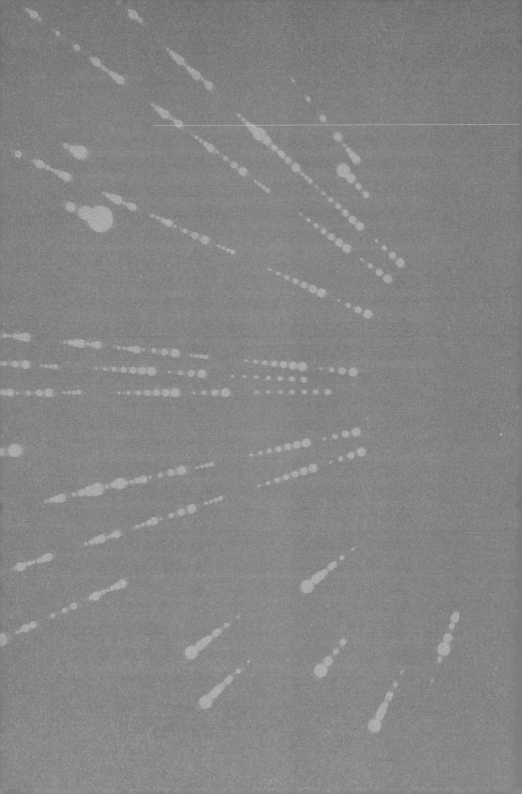

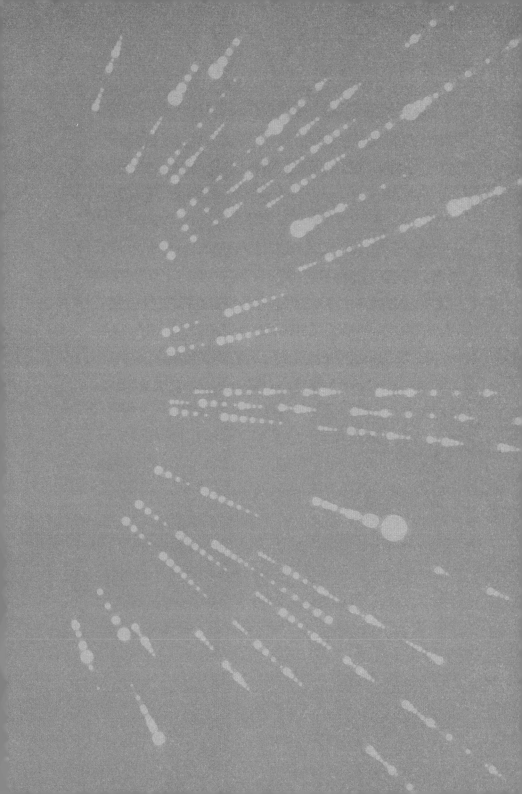